TAKE SELF OUT OF SELF PUBLISHING

INDEPENDENT AUTHOR'S GUIDE

PRINCESS F. L. GOODEN

Copyright © 2025 by Princess F. L. Gooden

ISBN: 9798282808803

All rights reserved.

No part of this book may be reproduced in any form or by any electronic or mechanical means, including information storage and retrieval systems, without written permission from the author, except for the use of brief quotations in a book review.

If I can help someone along the way…

Then my living won't be in vain.

To all of the people who took my advice and it worked.

CONTENTS

Introduction — 9

I. PRE-WRITING & PLANNING MISTAKES

DO NOT Try To Appeal To Everyone — 15
DO NOT Sacrifice Authenticity For Trends — 23
DO NOT Skip Outlining — 29
DO NOT Chase Trends Over Passion — 35
DO NOT Skip Research — 39
DO NOT Build Weak Fictional Worlds — 45
DO NOT Risk Lawsuits With Real Characters — 49
DO NOT Write Without Deadlines — 55

II. WRITING & MANUSCRIPT DEVELOPMENT MISTAKES

DO NOT Create Flat Antagonists — 61
DO NOT Publish First Drafts — 65
DO NOT Rely On AI Without Review — 69
DO NOT Overuse Passive Voice — 75
DO NOT Mix Tenses — 81
DO NOT Write Fake Dialogue — 87
DO NOT Switch Viewpoints Randomly — 91
DO NOT Info-Dump — 99
DO NOT Neglect Character Development — 105
DO NOT Start Slowly — 111
DO NOT Avoid Emotional Depth — 115
DO NOT End Without Resolution — 121
DO NOT Ignore Emotional Stakes — 125
DO NOT Add Pointless Subplots — 129
DO NOT Explain Everything — 133

III. EDITING & REVISION MISTAKES

DO NOT Ignore Beta Reader Feedback	139
DO NOT Skip Professional Editing or Dismiss Feedback	145
DO NOT Rely Only On Grammar Tools	153
DO NOT Cut Corners On Presentation: Proofreading and Formatting Matter	159
DO NOT Rewrite Indefinitely	167
DO NOT Publish With Inconsistencies	173

IV. COVER DESIGN & BOOK FORMATTING MISTAKES

DO NOT Neglect Spine And Back Cover	181
DO NOT Choose Illegible Fonts	187
DO NOT Design Your Own Cover or Use Amateur Images	193
DO NOT Violate Font Licenses	199
DO NOT Send Mixed Visual Messages: Cover Design That Sells	205
DO NOT Skip Professional Proof Copies	213
DO NOT Choose Odd Trim Sizes	221
DO NOT Use Unlicensed Stock Images	227
DO NOT Forget Your Copyright Page	229

V. LEGAL & BUSINESS MISTAKES

DO NOT Risk Your Work or Use Others' Content Illegally	235
DO NOT Ignore Tax Implications	243
DO NOT Ignore the Business of Being an Author	249
DO NOT Ignore Piracy	257
DO NOT Invent Author Identities Without Research	265
DO NOT Skip Business Insurance	271
DO NOT Work Without Contracts	275
DO NOT Ignore Privacy Regulations	283
DO NOT Overlook Subsidiary Rights	289

VI. PUBLISHING & DISTRIBUTION MISTAKES

DO NOT Price Emotionally	297
DO NOT Accept Free ISBNs Blindly	303
DO NOT Publish In One Format Only	309
DO NOT Miss Pre-Order Opportunities	319
DO NOT Rush To Publish	325
DO NOT Overlook Bulk Sales	331
DO NOT Ignore Seasonal Timing	337
DO NOT Forget Special Editions	343
DO NOT Waste Serial Rights	349

VII. MARKETING & PROMOTION MISTAKES

DO NOT Write Generic Author Bios	357
DO NOT Assume Books Sell Themselves	361
DO NOT Spam Readers with Book Links	365
DO NOT Rely On Occasional Social Posts	371
DO NOT Avoid Paid Advertising	379
DO NOT Ignore Discoverability: Metadata, Keywords, and Alternative Sales Channels	387
DO NOT Abandon Your Author Website	393
DO NOT Neglect To Build A Reader Community	399
DO NOT Wait For Media To Discover Your Book	405
DO NOT Buy Fake Reviews	411
DO NOT Argue With Reviewers	415
DO NOT Use Misleading Advertising	419
DO NOT Underestimate Book Trailers	425
DO NOT Ignore Goodreads	429
DO NOT Expect Signing Success Without Promotion	431
DO NOT Ignore Analytics	437
DO NOT Stop Marketing	443
DO NOT Miss Opportunities For Face-To-Face Promotion	449

VIII. MINDSET & BUSINESS GROWTH MISTAKES

DO NOT Forget You're Building a Career   457
DO NOT Avoid Author Networking   465

THE END

DO Not Say "The End" if you're not finished   477

INTRODUCTION

FROM MY HEART TO YOURS

I started a publishing company two years after becoming a published author in 2014. Then in March 2025, I quit. Not by choice, initially—my entire team quit first. They'd simply had enough. We genuinely loved bringing self-published authors' dreams to life, but the majority of those authors transformed our dreams into nightmares.

We invested in education, stayed current on industry trends, and mastered efficient publishing methods. None of that mattered when authors refused to listen. Somehow, we ended up more invested in their books than they were themselves.

If you already know what to do, why hire someone? And if you've hired an expert, throwing away money by ignoring their advice makes zero sense. This contradiction haunted our business. Authors would pay for expertise, then fight us at

INTRODUCTION

every turn—treating professional recommendations as optional suggestions.

The pattern was predictable: initial excitement on both sides, followed by resistance. Authors would question edits, challenge marketing advice, or ignore crucial recommendations. These weren't bad people; they were caught in a psychological trap. Having invested some money—but not a painful amount—they remained half-committed, unwilling to fully surrender to professional guidance.

Our affordable pricing created an unintended problem. We kept rates low to help authors succeed without breaking their banks. That was our miscalculation. The affordability masked our professional-grade quality. Authors saw our rates and categorized our services as "budget" rather than "investment."

People don't respect what they don't pay much for. When clients invested less financially, they invested less emotionally. When you charge $500 for something worth $2,000, clients don't think they're getting a steal—they think you're providing $500 quality.

I wrote this book not as a disgruntled publisher's rant, but because I genuinely want to help. By sharing these insights directly, I can reconnect with my authentic voice while offering unfiltered guidance.

You have to take the "self" out of "self-publishing" to truly succeed. Effective publishing requires professional distance and expertise that most authors simply don't possess.

INTRODUCTION

The "self" component is the indie industry's biggest deception. Once you decide to share your words, it stops being about you. It becomes about your readers, your business, your legacy. And doing everything yourself is extremely far-fetched.

I launched my first book in 2010 with no coach, editor, cover designer, or marketing plan—just excitement and the naive belief that good writing would sell itself. I sold exactly 12 copies, 10 to family members. That failure taught me more than success ever could. It forced me to confront the uncomfortable truth: the "self" needed to take a backseat.

I invested in learning from professionals, took courses, joined anthology projects, and created book covers while learning what sells. Each lesson pulled me further from the romantic notion of the solitary artist and closer to understanding publishing as a professional industry with established best practices. When I stopped treating my books like personal treasures and started seeing them as market commodities, my career shifted. My sales jumped. My audience expanded. Publishing houses reached out.

The most painful lesson? Nobody cares about your book as much as you do. Not your spouse. Not your best friend. Certainly not strangers scrolling through Amazon. They care about what your book can do for them.

I've watched countless talented writers crash because they couldn't separate ego from work. Your manuscript isn't your baby—it's your product. This isn't about art for art's sake. It's about creating something people will exchange money to read.

INTRODUCTION

I no longer want to sell "fish." It's time I taught you how to fish for yourself. What qualifies me? My failures—not my successes. My failures forced me to study market trends, consumer psychology, and publishing economics like my career depended on it—because it did.

This isn't a feel-good guide full of empty encouragement. This is the tough conversation not many will have with you. The one where I tell you exactly what's holding you back from creating a book that actually sells.

I refuse to sugarcoat anything. The publishing world transforms constantly. What drove sales five years back could be useless today. You need fresh, implementable tactics that deliver results now.

Taking the "self" out of self-publishing isn't about losing your voice—it's about gaining the objective perspective and business acumen necessary to transform your manuscript from a personal passion project into a marketable product readers will actually buy. This is your roadmap to publishing not just as an author, but as a professional who understands what it truly takes to succeed in today's ever-changing literary landscape.

I. PRE-WRITING & PLANNING MISTAKES

DO NOT TRY TO APPEAL TO EVERYONE

The Reader Partnership: Building the Foundation of Your Success

Your book isn't for everyone. Let that sink in. Feel the pushback rising in your chest. That inner voice protesting, *"But my message speaks to everyone! All readers could benefit from my words!"* I know that voice. I've listened to it. I've obeyed it. It's a lie.

The Reader Contract That Makes or Breaks Your Book

When readers pick up a book, they're entering into an unspoken agreement with you. They have specific expectations based on genre signals, cover design, and marketing promises. Break this agreement, and they won't just be disappointed—they'll feel betrayed.

That romance novel without a happy ending? It wasn't a romance novel at all. Period. No matter the author's claims, the beautiful love story, or the well-crafted prose—without that happily-ever-after, it's just fiction with romantic elements. And the readers weren't just disappointed—they were furious.

Breaking genre expectations isn't innovation. It's breaking a promise to your audience. This isn't theoretical—it's marketplace reality, where reader trust is the only currency that matters.

One author crashed and burned after publishing a "mystery thriller" that revealed the killer in chapter three. They thought they were "subverting expectations" and "creating something fresh." What they were actually doing? Disrespecting readers' time, money, and emotional investment.

The Temptation of Universal Appeal

When I released my first indie book, I thought I was being smart—writing for anyone struggling with dishonesty. It sounded inclusive. It sounded helpful. I convinced myself my book was for everyone because everyone bends the truth sometimes.

I was avoiding the hard work of making a choice. I was dodging specificity, running from clarity, and evading the need to define exactly who would benefit from my book the most. And the result? When you try to reach everyone, you end up reaching no one.

Non-Negotiable Genre Elements

When a reader picks up your book, they expect certain non-negotiable elements:

- Romance demands a happily-ever-after or happy-for-now ending
- Mysteries require crime resolution and fair-play clues
- Thrillers need escalating tension and high stakes
- Fantasy must maintain consistent magical systems and world rules
- Horror should deliver genuine fear or dread
- Self-help requires actionable advice and proof of expertise

These aren't arbitrary rules but foundations—the solid ground beneath creative expression. Like architectural principles preventing building collapse, genre conventions prevent reader disappointment.

The Power of Recognition

Think about it—when was the last time you picked up a book because it was meant for "everyone"? When did you last feel deeply seen by content created for "whoever might be interested"?

Never.

You chose that book because it spoke directly to your struggle, your ambition, your situation. It recognized you. That's what your readers crave. Not watered-down wisdom for the masses. Not vague insights that apply to everyone but resonate with no one. They need your distinct voice speaking straight to their circumstances.

Finding Your True Audience

So, ask yourself:

- Who lies awake at night with the problem I solve?
- Who has the specific passion, pain, or interest my book addresses?
- Who will feel instantly understood when they read my first page?

That's your audience.

Maybe it's:

- Working mothers balancing career ambition with family responsibility
- Fantasy readers who crave complex moral dilemmas over simple good vs. evil
- Mid-career professionals facing burnout in corporate environments
- Urban homesteaders seeking practical sustainability solutions
- Mystery lovers who enjoy academic settings and intellectual puzzles

Blending Genres Successfully

Creating a rom-com thriller? You must deliver:

- The romantic happy ending readers expect (romance)
- Humor that lightens tension (comedy)

- Genuine threat and escalating stakes (thriller)

Building a fantasy murder mystery? Ensure:

- A consistent magical system (fantasy)
- Fair-play clues solvable within that system (mystery)
- A satisfying resolution that honors both genre expectations

Even in genre blending, one must lead—clearly signaled through cover design, blurb, and marketing. In physical bookstores, novels sit in one section, not five.

Is it primarily fantasy with mystery elements? Or a mystery set in a fantasy world? This distinction isn't semantic—it's a promise. The dominant genre establishes which expectations cannot be broken, while secondary elements add layers but ultimately defer to the primary promise when tensions arise.

The Consequences of Vagueness

Here's what happens when you don't identify your audience:

Your marketing feels aimless because it has no clear target. Your book cover confuses potential readers because it's trying to appeal to everyone. Your writing lacks depth because depth requires focus. Your book sales plateau because readers can't recognize themselves in your message.

When you break genre promises, readers don't just stop reading—they leave reviews warning others away. They feel misled, not pleasantly surprised. They won't "appreciate your artistic vision" or "get over their expectations." They'll move on to authors who respect the genre enough to understand its foundations.

The Rewards of Specificity

But when you know who you're speaking to and what promises you're making, everything changes.

Your words carry weight because they address real struggles. Your marketing captivates because it reflects readers back to themselves. Your book stands out because it speaks directly to someone, not vaguely to everyone. Your audience grows because when people feel understood, they share your work.

Stop trying to be everything to everyone. Be everything to someone.

Honor the reader contract. Deliver on genre promises. Speak to specific readers with specific needs.

Because readers aren't seeking literary revolution. They're seeking their next favorite book in the genres they already love. Your desire to stand out shouldn't prevent you from serving the readers who came specifically for that promised experience.

Beyond Your Inner Circle

Your ideal reader isn't necessarily your spouse, your best friend, or your mama. Your ideal reader is the person who needs your insights, your perspective, your solution—whether they know you or not.

A productivity coach isn't writing for other coaches. They're writing for that overwhelmed CEO drowning in notifications.

A wellness author isn't targeting industry peers. They're speaking to that exhausted parent who can't find a moment to breathe.

The genre-specific elements that might seem limiting to you are exactly what make readers feel at home. When readers get what they expect—whether that's the romantic resolution, the mystery solution, or the promised transformation—they don't feel constrained by convention. They feel satisfied by promises kept.

Your readers are waiting. Not for a revolutionary book that breaks all the rules. Not for a universal message that speaks vaguely to everyone. They're waiting for the book that sees them specifically, understands them deeply, and delivers exactly what it promises.

DO NOT SACRIFICE AUTHENTICITY FOR TRENDS

The Myth of Total Originality vs. The Trap of Trend-Chasing

"It's never been done before."

Those five words have crushed more publishing dreams than bad writing ever could.

Picture this: You're pitching your book, eyes bright with excitement as you describe your "groundbreaking" premise. With your whole heart, you declare: "There's nothing else like it out there."

Stop. Breathe.

Your story isn't original. And that's completely okay.

At the other extreme is the author constantly checking bestseller lists, calculator in hand, trying to reverse-engineer success. They're analyzing trends, keywords, and cover designs with one goal: finding the fastest path to profit.

Their manuscript will never be finished. Or worse—it will be. A hollow thing born of market research instead of meaning. A book that checks all the boxes but touches no hearts. A product without a pulse.

The Originality Paradox

Every story builds on what came before. The popular wizarding school stories of today have roots in educational adventures written decades ago. Today's psychological thrillers evolved from noir fiction of the past. Even post-apocalyptic literature has a rich history dating back centuries.

I learned this lesson the hard way. After typing "The End" on a manuscript I'd worked on for a year, I called a fellow author to celebrate. As I described the plot, she casually mentioned, "That sounds like a film I watched a few months ago." Something deep and painful churned inside me.

Then I realized: Successful stories about survival competitions weren't the first to explore such territory. Popular paranormal romances built upon centuries of folklore and gothic traditions. Bestselling religious conspiracy thrillers followed paths blazed by earlier works.

What burns the most successful books into our collective memory isn't their novel concepts. It's their genuine voice and perspective.

The Market-Chasing Trap

Somewhere right now, someone is staring at bestseller lists, calculator in hand, trying to reverse-engineer success. They're analyzing trends, keywords, and cover designs with one goal: finding the fastest path to profit.

I abandoned my first novel after months of chasing market trends instead of following the story that haunted my dreams. The characters moved like puppets, their strings visible with every forced plot twist. Their voices rang hollow because they weren't speaking from the heart—they were reciting formulas.

A bestseller means your book found readers at a particular moment. It means your marketing worked. It means you hit a wave at the right time. But it doesn't necessarily mean you created something lasting or moved souls.

Where True Originality Lives

Your uniqueness isn't in your plot—it's in how you tell it:

- Your perspective shaped by unique life experiences
- Your voice that carries distinctive rhythms and cadences
- Your specific thematic obsessions that emerge across your work
- Your emotional truth that resonates with readers on a human level

Two books with identical premises will feel entirely different depending on who writes them. One might feel like a casual conversation with a friend; the other like stepping into someone's most intimate thoughts.

The Cost of Writing Solely for Profit

When you write only for profit:

- Your characters sound like marketing personas
- Your plot twists feel mechanically inserted rather than naturally developed
- Your emotional scenes ring hollow or manipulative
- Your voice becomes generic, attempting to mimic successful writers
- Your creative joy evaporates, making it harder to finish

Market Awareness Isn't Evil

Understanding your market means:

- Knowing what readers expect from your genre
- Recognizing where to push boundaries and where to meet expectations
- Understanding how to position your work for discovery
- Crafting marketing that reaches genuine readers

These aren't creative shackles—they're tools to help your story find its readers.

Your Path to Success Requires Both Heart and Head

Start with passion:

- What story keeps you awake at night?
- What characters haunt you until you give them life?
- What question or theme feels too important to leave unexplored?
- What story would you write even if no one ever read it?

That's your starting point.

Then apply market intelligence:

- Study successful books in your genre
- Understand reader expectations
- Learn proper formatting and presentation
- Create professional packaging

Long-term bestsellers—books that keep selling years after launch—share common elements:

- Authentic passion for the subject
- Professional-grade execution
- Market-aware positioning
- Distinctive voice

Finding Clarity in Your Creative Direction

The most successful books aren't those chasing trends or doggedly pursuing absolute originality. They're the ones where authors:

1. Write from authentic passion and interest
2. Execute with professional craft and skill
3. Position with market awareness
4. Present with distinctive voice and perspective

Your stories and ideas don't need to be utterly original—they just need to be authentically yours. Your market knowledge shouldn't dictate what you write—it should help what you write find its readers.

Write what matters to you. Make it as good as it can be. Then, and only then, figure out how to sell it. Money is a result, not a reason. Your readers can tell the difference between a book written for profit and a book written with purpose. In the long run, they'll reward the one that speaks to their soul, not their search terms.

The key isn't finding an idea no one has ever thought of—it's bringing your unique perspective to ideas that have always mattered. And it isn't chasing whatever's trending this week—it's creating work with enough authentic passion that it remains meaningful long after the trends have shifted.

DO NOT SKIP OUTLINING

The Power of Planning Your Manuscript

That unfinished manuscript? It's gathering dust because you didn't plan it properly and you never defined its purpose. You started strong with characters that felt alive and scenes that played like movies. Then you hit the void—that moment when you had no idea where to go next. The inspiration dried up. Your characters went silent. The path disappeared.

"But I'm a pantser!" you protest. "I write by the seat of my pants!"

Your Story Needs a Map

An outline isn't a cage—it's a compass. And there's no "proper" outline. Your outline might be:

- Three sentences on a napkin about beginning, middle, and end

- Character arcs mapped in a notebook
- Plot points on index cards across your floor
- A detailed chapter-by-chapter breakdown
- Voice memos recorded while driving

The "pantser versus plotter" debate is overrated. It's been the downfall of more books than writer's block ever could.

Learning from Chefs

Think about chefs. Even the masters follow recipes. Not because they lack creativity, but because recipes work. The recipe isn't constraining their genius—it's giving them a foundation. They experiment only after understanding what makes a dish succeed.

Writing works exactly the same way. Every "pantser" who finished a book had some kind of plan, even if just a destination. Every "plotter" who wrote something alive knew when to deviate from their outline and follow the story's heartbeat. What matters isn't how detailed your map is—it's that you have some idea of where you're going.

Try this: Take out paper. Write down what you know about your story. Not what you should know. Not what other writers would know. Just what YOU know right now.

That's your outline.

The "pantser versus plotter" question isn't about writing style—it's about fear. Fear of commitment. Fear of "getting it wrong." Fear of killing the magic. But real magic happens when your creativity has direction.

Your Book Needs a Reason to Exist

Every writer faces that moment when passion meets purpose. Those nighttime whispers. Characters walking beside you like shadows. Concepts unfolding like origami in your mind. They seduce you with their brilliance. But brilliance without direction is just a flash that disappears. Before writing another word, ask yourself: Why does this book need to exist?

This answer shapes everything: voice, structure, audience, impact.

Your purpose is a compass in a storm. When confusion threatens, when doubt circles, when fatigue makes every island look like home—your purpose points true north.

- "This book exists to help first-time homebuyers avoid costly mistakes."
- "This book exists to teach beginners to cook with confidence."
- "This book exists to help grieving parents find hope."
- "This book exists to show entrepreneurs how to scale sustainably."

Each purpose contains a universe in a sentence. It names who it serves. It promises transformation. It implies voice, structure, direction.

The Cost of Working Without Purpose

Without this clarity, your writing wanders. Scenes sprawl

without consequence. Characters act without meaning. Readers drift away, sensing the absence of intention.

When a writer anchors their work in purpose, each line pulls its weight. Every moment propels us toward answers. Each character illuminates the deeper message. Readers sense the sure grip of a writer who understands both destination and significance.

Many writers spend years on manuscripts—hundreds of pages of beautiful prose, vivid characters, intricate world-building. Each sentence polished until it gleams. Yet something is wrong. The story moves, but toward what? The characters evolve, but why? The world dazzles, but to what end? When an editor asks, "What is this book trying to say?" the writer has a dozen different answers. All insufficient.

Finding the true purpose might take months. Months of soul-searching about why this story demands to be told. When clarity arrives, it isn't constraining—it's liberating. Once you understand your core message, you can see which moments truly advance it and which are just beautiful distractions. You know which character arcs need more depth. You recognize exactly where the story needs to end.

The Two-Step Solution

The solution to finishing your manuscript comes down to two essential steps:

1. Create your map: Outline in whatever way works for you. Use whatever tools help you see the path. Trust that your creativity is stronger than any plan—it can always take you somewhere better. Just don't start without some idea of where you're going.

2. Define your purpose: Before you commit your vision to the page, complete this sentence: "This book exists to..." Make your answer specific without being small. Ambitious without being impossible. Name those you seek to serve. Promise transformation worth the journey.

Purpose isn't just about what you want to say—it's about what your readers need. It's about the change your words will create in the world. Your readers are waiting for the book only you can write. Not just any book. The necessary book. The purposeful book. The book that fills a void they perhaps didn't even know existed until your words illuminated it.

DO NOT CHASE TRENDS OVER PASSION

Somewhere right now, someone is staring at Amazon's bestseller lists, calculator in hand, trying to reverse-engineer success. They're analyzing trends, keywords, and cover designs with one goal: finding the fastest path to profit.

Their manuscript will never be finished. Or worse—it will be. A hollow thing born of market research instead of meaning. A book that checks all the boxes but touches no hearts. A product without a pulse.

I abandoned my first novel after months of chasing market trends instead of following the story that haunted my dreams. The characters moved like puppets, their strings visible with every forced plot twist. Their voices rang hollow because they weren't speaking from the heart—they were reciting formulas.

What "Bestseller" Really Means

A bestseller means your book found readers at a particular moment. It means your marketing worked. It means you hit a wave at the right time. But it doesn't necessarily mean you created something lasting or moved souls.

Some of our most beloved books never hit a bestseller list. Some bestsellers are forgotten within months. The market rewards many things, and quality is only one of them.

The Balance: Market Awareness Without Creative Compromise

Understanding your market isn't evil. It means:

- Knowing what readers expect from your genre
- Recognizing where to push boundaries and where to meet expectations
- Understanding how to position your work for discovery
- Crafting marketing that reaches genuine readers

These aren't creative shackles—they're tools to help your story find its readers.

Finding Your Balance: The Heart and Mind of Successful Writing

Start with passion:

- What story keeps you awake at night?
- What characters haunt you until you give them life?

- What question or theme feels too important to leave unexplored?
- What story would you write even if no one ever read it?

That's your starting point.

Then apply market intelligence:

- Study successful books in your genre
- Understand reader expectations
- Learn proper formatting and presentation
- Create professional packaging

The Elements of Enduring Success

Long-term bestsellers—books that keep selling years after launch—share common elements:

- Authentic passion for the subject
- Professional-grade execution
- Market-aware positioning
- Distinctive voice

Your Passion Is Your Fuel

It will:

- Sustain you through difficult drafts
- Give your work the authenticity readers crave

- Push you to excellence when "good enough" would suffice
- Create the kind of book people press into friends' hands

The most successful authors aren't those who chase trends or ignore the market entirely—they're the ones who bring their passion to the page, then do the work to help that passion find its readers. Write what matters to you. Make it as good as it can be. Then, and only then, figure out how to sell it. Money is a result, not a reason.

Your readers can tell the difference between a book written for profit and a book written with purpose. In the long run, they'll reward the one that speaks to their soul, not their search terms.

DO NOT SKIP RESEARCH

Your Experience Isn't Enough

Your story matters. Your experience is valid. Your perspective is unique. But it's not enough. Personal experience isn't enough. Your memory fails you. What you know today becomes outdated tomorrow.

Think about this: doctors spend years in medical school and they are still required to research before every procedure. They can't rely solely on what worked last time. They verify. They update. They cross-reference. Each patient is different. Each situation is unique. Your readers deserve that same level of respect.

Efficient Research Methodologies for Time Pressed Authors

Effective research doesn't mean endless months in libraries. Use these targeted approaches:

The Progressive Depth Method

- Start with broad overview sources
- Identify key knowledge gaps
- Dive deeper only on essential topics
- Verify critical information with expert sources

This structured approach prevents both superficial research and endless rabbit holes.

The 5/25/100 Research Framework

- 5 hours on broad topic exploration
- 25 sources for general understanding
- 100 focused minutes on critical facts

This creates sufficient depth while maintaining practical boundaries.

The Research Sprint Technique

- Set specific research questions
- Establish firm time boundaries
- Work in focused 25-minute intervals
- Document findings immediately

This prevents endless browsing while maintaining momentum.

Evaluating Source Credibility in an Era of Misinformation

Not all sources deserve equal weight. Apply these evaluation criteria:

The TRACCS Credibility Assessment Framework

- Timeliness: How recent is the information?
- Reputation: What's the source's standing in its field?
- Authority: What are the author's credentials?
- Corroboration: Do other reliable sources agree?
- Clarity: Is the information presented clearly?
- Scope: Does the source cover the topic thoroughly?

Red Flags for Unreliable Sources

- Lack of citations or references
- Excessive claims or promises
- Heavy reliance on anecdotes rather than data
- Conflict of interest or hidden agenda
- Outdated information presented as current

The Triangulation Method

For critical facts, always find three independent sources that confirm the information. If you can't find three reliable sources, mark the information as tentative or reconsider including it.

Organizing Research for Maximum Usability

The difference between drowning in research and using it effectively is organization:

The ATLAS Research Organization System

- Aggregate: Collect information in one place

- Tag: Create searchable categories
- Link: Connect related information
- Annotate: Add your insights
- Summarize: Create quick-reference notes

Digital Organization Tools

- Research databases like Zotero or Mendeley
- Note systems like Evernote or Notion
- Mind-mapping software for visual thinkers
- Citation managers for academic work

Physical Organization for Visual Thinkers

- Index cards for key facts
- Bulletin boards for connecting ideas
- Color-coding for themes or topics
- Dedicated research journals

Primary vs. Secondary Research: When to Use Each

Both approaches have distinct value in nonfiction:

Primary Research Methods

- Interviews with experts and subjects
- Surveys and questionnaires
- Direct observations and experiments
- Original document analysis

Primary research provides:

- Unique insights not available elsewhere
- Fresh perspectives on established topics
- Credibility through direct engagement
- Material that differentiates your book

Secondary Research Methods

- Academic journals and books
- Reputable news sources
- Government and institutional publications
- Industry reports and white papers

Secondary research provides:

- Established facts and consensus views
- Historical context and background
- Theoretical frameworks
- Expert opinions beyond your network

Balancing Primary and Secondary Research

For most nonfiction books, aim for:

- 30-40% original research (interviews, surveys, etc.)
- 60-70% validated secondary sources
- At least 3-5 expert interviews per major topic
- Secondary verification of personal experiences

This balance creates books that contribute something new while standing on solid foundations.

The Research-Writing Integration Process

Research isn't separate from writing—it's intertwined:

The Spiral Method

1. Begin with basic research
2. Write initial content
3. Identify knowledge gaps
4. Research specific questions
5. Revise with new information
6. Repeat until complete

This prevents both research paralysis and premature writing.

Remember: Your readers trust you to be their guide. They invest time, money, and faith in your words. Every fact, claim, and piece of advice needs to be rock-solid.

Your book deserves the depth that comes from proper research. Your readers deserve the confidence that comes from accurate information. Your reputation depends on the credibility that only thorough research can provide.

DO NOT BUILD WEAK FICTIONAL WORLDS

Picture your favorite novel. The one that felt so real you could touch it, taste it, breathe it. The one that made you forget you were reading words on a page. That wasn't an accident. That was world-building.

World-building isn't just for fantasy and science fiction. Every story happens somewhere. Every character lives in a world. When that world is weak, the entire narrative collapses.

The Cost of Weak Worlds

In a weak world:

- Characters feel disconnected from their environment
- Plot points lack logical consequences
- Readers struggle to suspend disbelief
- Emotional impact diminishes
- Story logic falls apart

Many authors learn this lesson the hard way. One writer crafted a woman's emotional return to her coastal hometown with painstaking character development but sketched the surroundings with lazy strokes—generic beaches, nameless streets, a town that could have been anywhere. The rejection letters all pointed to the same problem: disconnection from environment, lack of specificity, and an unbelievable world.

The Interconnected Nature of Worlds

Remember: Every aspect affects every other aspect. If magic exists, it impacts warfare, medicine, communication, access to power, and religious beliefs. When technology advances, traditional skills become obsolete, power dynamics shift, and new ethical questions emerge.

World-Building Requirements

Your world must have:

- Internal consistency and logic
- Sensory specificity (sights, sounds, smells, textures, tastes)
- Cultural systems (values, taboos, traditions)
- Economic realities (how people survive, class structures)
- Physical laws (whether natural or supernatural)
- Historical context (events that shaped the present)
- Environmental influence (how geography shapes culture)

Consider a grandmother's kitchen: the worn wooden spoon hanging from a nail, flour-dusted cookbook open to the same page, the precise angle of sunlight that signals breadmaking time. That's not just setting—it's a world with rules, rhythms, and history.

Essential Questions to Ask

- How do people meet their basic needs (food, shelter, safety)?
- What power structures exist and how are they maintained?
- What do people value, fear, and believe?
- How do environment and resources shape daily life?
- What technologies or capabilities exist and who controls them?
- What historical events shaped the current situation?
- What conflicts naturally arise from your world's structure?

Document your decisions—both major and minor. Create a world bible and track your details. Inconsistencies pull readers out faster than bad grammar ever could.

Integration, Not Information Dumps

Your world exists to serve your story, not overshadow it. Reveal your world through:

- Character interactions with environment
- Dialogue that reflects cultural norms

- Conflict arising from world conditions
- Sensory details that orient readers
- Character assumptions that reveal normalcy
- Small moments that illuminate larger systems

The best world-building doesn't feel like world-building. It feels like life.

Readers need to believe in your world before they can believe in your story. You're not just telling a story—you're creating a world for your story to live in. Make it strong enough to support everything you build upon it.

DO NOT RISK LAWSUITS WITH REAL CHARACTERS

That family drama would make a perfect book. The office scandal is too juicy not to share. Your ex's behavior belongs in a cautionary tale.

Stop.

Put down the keyboard.

That perfect story could land you in perfect legal trouble.

A legal section appears later in this book, but this information can't wait until the end. Readers need to understand these crucial details before using any publication to express personal insights, challenge others, or share their experiences.

Real Stories, Real Consequences

Di'Shay (not her real name) wrote a "fictional" account of workplace harassment, changing names but keeping her real company's culture. She thought that was enough protection.

She was wrong. She preserved her boss's distinctive glasses, his unusual meeting-ending ritual, a specific coffee incident at the company retreat, and their unique office layout.

Result? Legal threats. Pulled publication. Lost money.

Then there's Dante', who published a memoir exposing his mother's addiction, father's financial failures, sister's eating disorder, and private family secrets. He didn't ask permission. Didn't change details. Didn't consider privacy rights.

Result? Family lawsuit. Destroyed relationships. Books destroyed.

The weather turned suddenly that afternoon, the sky darkening as Desmond pulled into his parents' driveway. The certified letter from his sister's attorney sat on the passenger seat—its official language demanding six figures in damages, immediate end to book sales, and public retraction.

His memoir had existed just eleven days. Eleven days of seeing his name on a spine, watching his Amazon ranking, imagining readers finally understanding his struggles. Eleven days of validation before everything collapsed.

He simply wanted to share his story.

He failed to realize that his story was also legally connected to others.

The Legal Reality

Changing names isn't enough when:

- The person is identifiable through specific traits, habits, or experiences
- You include unique incidents that others could recognize
- The portrayal includes private information not publicly available
- Physical characteristics, speech patterns, or mannerisms remain distinctive

What triggers lawsuits:

- Defamation (false statements that damage reputation)
- Invasion of privacy (revealing private facts)
- Misappropriation (using someone's identity for commercial gain)
- Intentional infliction of emotional distress
- False light (misleading portrayals that cause harm)

Legally protected elements include:

- Personal identifying information and likeness
- Private facts not in public record
- Professional reputation
- Family relationships and private conduct
- Personal history and experiences

Protecting Yourself

To avoid legal disaster:

- Create composite characters that blend multiple real people
- Change significant identifying details (age, appearance, background)
- Alter locations, timelines, and specific incidents
- Get written permission when using recognizable real people
- Have a qualified attorney review your manuscript
- Consider liability insurance for published works

Real-world protections:

- Disclaimers help show intent but don't prevent lawsuits
- "Based on a true story" doesn't provide legal immunity
- "All characters fictional" statements don't protect against identifiable portrayals
- Fiction labels don't shield you from legal consequences
- Truth is a defense for defamation but not privacy violations

Real-Life Consequences

In her apartment, Deborah stared at the cease-and-desist letter, throat tight with disbelief. The publisher's email had followed minutes later—they were pulling her book. Effective immediately. All those nights parsing words and polishing sentences, destroyed by a single legal document.

"But I changed the names," she whispered to the empty room. "I called it fiction."

The lawyer explained it gently: fiction wasn't a magic shield. Her character still had her former boss's distinctive limp, his habit of quoting obscure philosophers, his custom-made desk that anyone who'd worked there would recognize instantly.

She'd wanted to expose the facts. Instead, she'd exposed herself to legal consequences she couldn't afford.

Essential Protection Strategies

Just because something actually happened doesn't mean you can write about it freely. People's private lives are legally protected, no matter how badly you want to tell their story. Your good intentions won't save you in court. What matters is how your words affect others, not what you meant by them.

Your story matters. But tell it safely. Tell it legally. Tell it without risking everything.

Get legal advice. Get written permissions. Get it right.

Your career depends on it.

DO NOT WRITE WITHOUT DEADLINES

The Ghost of Unfinished Manuscripts

A promising novel once lived in fragments across five years of Princess's life. Not because it demanded extensive research, but because she treated writing like it belonged to a mystical realm where inspiration descended only when the stars aligned. She wrote in passionate bursts that burned hot for days, then vanished for months, leaving characters suspended in literary purgatory.

Her reckoning came during a family gathering when her uncle asked about "that book" she'd been talking about for years. His voice casual, his eyes anything but. In that moment, the weight of all her unfinished promises collapsed into a single, unbearable realization—she didn't believe she'd ever finish. Neither did anyone else.

That night, alone with this revelation, she made a commitment that felt both small and seismic: 500 words a day, no exceptions, no excuses. Not because she suddenly had more time, but because she finally understood that waiting for the perfect moment meant waiting forever.

The unfinished manuscript haunts every writer who's ever whispered, "I'll get to it when..." It's the brilliant idea never materialized, the promising draft abandoned midway, the revision eternally postponed. Writers convince themselves that real writing happens in bursts of inspiration, that structure would somehow diminish the art.

This is a dangerous lie.

Without clear goals and deadlines, a writing life becomes a landscape of good intentions leading nowhere. Days between writing sessions stretch into weeks. Weeks bleed into months. Characters once known intimately become strangers whose motivations are forgotten. Plot threads unravel. Voice shifts. The book takes months longer than necessary—sometimes years, sometimes forever.

The words "I'm working on a book" eventually carry the hollow ring of empty promises. Each time they're spoken, something inside grows smaller, quieter.

Ask yourself: How many started-but-abandoned projects sit in your drawer or hard drive? How many ideas have withered because you never gave them structure to grow? How many times have you described your book in the perpetual present tense, never reaching the past tense of completion?

Writing without goals is like crossing an ocean with no compass—you might drift forward briefly, but you'll eventually lose direction.

Facing the Inevitable Obstacles

When you say, "I don't have time," what you're really saying is, "I haven't decided this matters enough yet." Even fifteen minutes a day, protected like a small flame, can eventually grow into the fire of a finished book.

When procrastination takes hold, shrink the task until it no longer feels overwhelming. Don't aim to write a chapter—write a paragraph. Don't write for an hour—write for ten minutes. Make the task so small that your resistance has nothing to cling to.

When motivation fades, turn to your visual reminders. Look at the calendar with its marked squares. Read through your journal entries. Remember why you started, what truth you're telling, and who needs to hear it.

When inspiration feels absent, write anyway. Here's the secret of professional writers: momentum creates inspiration more reliably than inspiration creates momentum. You don't wait for the muse—you summon her by showing up every day.

The blank page will always be intimidating. The middle of a manuscript will always feel like a forest with paths that disappear. Revisions will always reveal the distance between what you've written and what you hope to create. These aren't signs that you're failing—they're signs that you're writing.

Writing isn't just art—it's practice. It isn't just expression—it's commitment. It isn't just talent—it's the decision, made over and over, that this matters enough to keep going.

Three months after that family gathering reckoning, Princess's once-stalled novel had a completed first draft. Not because of a sudden burst of genius. Not because inspiration struck like a lightning bolt. But because she understood that books aren't written through talent or luck or divine intervention.

They're written through structure, consistency, and the quiet courage of showing up even when showing up feels impossible.

Set your goals. Honor your deadlines. And remember—this book you're working so hard to finish isn't just a collection of bound pages. It's proof that you chose yourself, your voice, your story—over the seductive comfort of "someday."

II. WRITING & MANUSCRIPT DEVELOPMENT MISTAKES

DO NOT CREATE FLAT ANTAGONISTS

A hero is only as strong as the obstacles they face. Nothing drains tension from a story faster than a weak antagonist. Readers don't want a generic bad guy—they demand someone compelling, someone who forces the protagonist to evolve.

Too many authors settle for cardboard cutout villains—the evil CEO, the vengeful ex, the monster who's "just bad." These flat characters don't challenge heroes in meaningful ways, making stories predictable and forgettable.

The Problem with Weak Antagonists

The first manuscript I edited professionally featured a villain so generic I couldn't remember his name between chapters. He lurked in shadows and plotted with such predictable malice that his scenes became skimmable. When I suggested adding complexity, the author seemed confused: "But he's the bad guy. Why does he need more than that?"

Because villains aren't plot devices—they're mirrors reflecting what the hero could become. They create the pressure that forms the diamond of your protagonist's character. When your villain lacks substance, your entire story loses weight, tension, and impact.

Signs Your Antagonist Isn't Strong Enough

I once worked with a fantasy author whose "Dark Lord" remained offstage for most of the novel, only to be swiftly defeated by a magical sword the hero acquired effortlessly. The author admitted, "I was more interested in my hero's journey than developing a complicated villain."

The truth? Your hero's journey is only as compelling as the force pushing against it.

Creating Stronger Antagonists

One of my clients transformed her thriller by developing the antagonist from a generic "crime boss" into a man who grew up in poverty alongside the hero. While the protagonist became a cop, the antagonist built a criminal empire that, in his mind, provided jobs and protection for people the system abandoned. Their final confrontation became both physical and ideological—two men who chose different paths to address the same injustice.

The rewritten climax wasn't just more exciting—it was heartbreaking because both believed they were right. Both had compelling reasons for their choices. Both represented valid responses to a broken system.

DO NOT CREATE FLAT ANTAGONISTS

Your protagonist deserves a worthy opponent. Your story deserves a conflict that keeps readers engaged. Your villain deserves to be more than a placeholder.

Give your antagonist depth, purpose, and strength, and watch your entire book transform.

DO NOT PUBLISH FIRST DRAFTS

First Drafts Are Not Final Drafts

There it is. "The End." Your heart races. Eyes mist. You've written an entire book and it feels perfect—raw, real, pure. You're terrified that editing will ruin the magic.

Every author knows this feeling. It's also the feeling that has killed thousands of potentially great books by pushing them into the world prematurely.

Finishing a first manuscript creates euphoria unlike any other. For many writers, the manuscript feels sacred—a testament to creativity and vulnerability. Changing a single word feels like sacrilege.

This is a dangerous illusion.

First drafts that get published without revision die quiet deaths on Amazon's back pages, buried under one-star reviews. They become cautionary tales whispered among writing groups. They haunt their creators for years—tangible evidence of impatience outweighing craft. They breed regret that intensifies with each year of writing experience.

Consider Reggie, who published his business book's first draft—complete with contradicting advice across chapters, faulty statistics, and examples that undermined his main points. A year later, trying to book speaking engagements, he kept hearing: "We looked at your book and..." His reputation was sealed by his impatience.

Or Richelle, whose romance novel featured a protagonist with changing eye colors, timeline inconsistencies, and abandoned plot threads. Her genuine talent disappeared behind avoidable errors, her reviews filled with complaints about poor editing rather than discussions of her creative voice.

First drafts capture passion but lack precision. They contain your authentic voice alongside verbal tics, repetitions, and crutch phrases. They hold your best ideas surrounded by unnecessary detours. They hide moments of brilliance under avoidable mistakes. The energy fueling first-draft writing is valuable, but it's just the beginning. It's a seed, not a garden.

Would you serve dinner guests uncooked ingredients? Would you perform a song you'd just written without practicing? Would you wear unfinished clothing with loose threads?

Your book deserves the same care.

The Revision Journey

Revision doesn't destroy your vision—it clarifies it. Think of sculptors: they don't stop with a rough shape. They refine. They polish. The statue already exists within the stone; revision reveals it.

Purposeful vs. Endless Revision

Necessary revision addresses specific weaknesses with clear goals:

- It improves clarity, consistency, and impact
- It makes your book more accessible to readers
- It enhances your core message and themes
- It strengthens character development and plot coherence
- It tightens pacing and eliminates redundancy

Endless tinkering stems from insecurity without direction:

- It moves sentences without improving meaning
- It becomes an excuse to avoid completion
- It focuses on perfection rather than progress
- It never ends because perfectionism has no finish line

The Strategic Approach to Revision

When approaching revision, create specific plans:

- Read aloud and mark where you stumble
- Create timelines to fix chronology issues

- Highlight repeated phrases and find fresh language
- Cut beautiful passages that don't serve the core narrative
- Create character consistency charts
- Map plot progression and fix structural issues
- Verify that each scene serves a clear purpose

The Emotional Reality of Revision

It will be excruciating. It will be liberating. It is necessary.

No reader has ever said, "I wish this book had been less polished."

The Promise of Quality

Your readers deserve your best work. Not your first work—your best work.

Give yourself permission to revise. To improve. To polish.

The magic isn't in the first draft—it's in the refinement. The greatest disservice you can do to your story is denying it the chance to become what it truly could be.

Your book deserves the time it takes to get it right.

DO NOT RELY ON AI WITHOUT REVIEW

The temptation is real. You need a book, but time is scarce. AI beckons with instant content. Ghostwriters promise bestsellers in weeks. These shortcuts seem like logical solutions.

They're not. They're reputation killers.

The Dangers of AI-Generated Content

A colleague once called me. A respected entrepreneur in our circle had become an industry joke overnight. His AI-generated business book was being systematically dismantled online—not for bad ideas, but for fabricated case studies, invented statistics, and contradictory advice that zigzagged between chapters.

"He never even read it," she told me. "Just fed AI an outline and published the output."

His decade of expertise evaporated. Rather than showcasing wisdom, he revealed his willingness to fake it. His name became synonymous with fraudulence.

This isn't an isolated case.

Take Tom. He copied AI output directly into his manuscript. Within months, readers identified contradictory advice, made-up statistics, fictional companies presented as real case studies, outdated information, and dangerous technical recommendations.

Or Elizabeth, who hired a ghostwriter but never carefully reviewed her "memoir." The result? Wrong family details, misrepresented events, scrambled timelines, fabricated dramatic moments, and missing cultural context that Elizabeth would have immediately caught had she bothered to read before approving.

The harsh reality: The ghostwriter didn't live your life. The AI didn't build your business. The writing tool didn't learn your hard lessons. Only you did.

Tools, Not Replacements

AI and ghostwriters are valuable tools—emphasis on tools. Like power equipment in a workshop, they can accelerate your project or cause catastrophic damage when misused.

The question isn't whether to use them. It's how to use them without surrendering what makes your book worth reading: you.

Using AI Effectively

- Use it for brainstorming when blocked
- Generate structural alternatives when stuck
- Get research suggestions (that you verify independently)
- Request organizational frameworks for complex information
- Solicit editing suggestions (that you evaluate against your voice)
- Always verify and rewrite in your voice. AI creates approximations based on patterns—not insights rooted in lived experience. It doesn't carry your wisdom or your journey.

Working With Ghostwriters

- Choose carefully—their understanding directly impacts authenticity
- Provide guidance about your message and your communication style
- Stay deeply involved throughout the writing process
- Review thoroughly—not skimming, but critical deep reading
- Maintain control of content direction
- Verify accuracy of technical details and personal stories
- Ensure the writing sounds like you at your best
- Understand every concept well enough to explain it yourself

Your responsibility begins, not ends, with hiring help.

The Authentication Framework

Content Verification

- Fact-check even minor details
- Validate all sources and quotes
- Confirm statistical claims
- Verify technical correctness
- Evaluate legal and ethical compliance
- Assess cultural sensitivity

Voice Authentication

- Integrate personal experiences throughout
- Include your unique perspective on familiar topics
- Maintain consistent style from start to finish
- Align tone with your authentic self
- Incorporate examples you can personally vouch for
- Share insights from your specific expertise

Quality Control

- Ensure logical flow between ideas
- Maintain argument coherence across chapters
- Verify examples actually support your points
- Confirm practical applicability of your advice
- Assess genuine value in every section
- Uphold professional standards in your field
- Guarantee industry accuracy

- Confirm original content without plagiarism risks

Your name on the cover means you own every word, every claim, every error. You're responsible for every consequence, criticism, and problem that arises.

This isn't perfectionism. It's integrity.

The Cost of Shortcuts

One of my clients experimented with AI for the technical sections where they struggled with clarity. The content appeared solid—comprehensive and well-structured. But when read aloud, it became clear: it didn't sound like them at all. The words were technically correct, but lacked emotion. They explained without creating a connection.

I watched them rebuild it from scratch, treating those AI passages like research notes instead of finished work. Sure, it meant more late nights and countless revisions, but what emerged was pure them - quirks, insights, and all the beautiful mess that makes their voice special.

That book? It's the one readers still message about. Not because every rough edge was polished, but because they allowed their authenticity to shine through every page.

The Protection Protocol

Read every word bearing your name. Verify every fact through independent sources. Check every claim against your actual knowledge. Test every suggestion to confirm effectiveness.

Validate every source. Own every idea by understanding it thoroughly enough to explain to a child.

Authenticity matters more than ever in a world flooded with synthetic content. Readers can spot inauthenticity instantly. Experts catch mistakes casual readers overlook. Critics highlight flaws in their reviews. Reality comes to light when advice falls short, and reputation fades with every exposed shortcut.

Use AI and ghostwriters wisely—for inspiration, not automation; assistance, not abdication; support, not substitution; ideas, not identity.

Your readers deserve your genuine expertise, voice, experience, insights, and perspective. They deserve validated content with your personal touch.

The book that takes longer but carries your genuine voice will outlast quick productions that offer nothing of you at all.

Don't sacrifice authenticity for speed. Don't trade credibility for convenience.

Your name. Your book. Your responsibility.

DO NOT OVERUSE PASSIVE VOICE

A story unfolds. Characters grow. Action explodes.

Feel the difference? That's active voice—direct, powerful, alive.

The Moment of Truth

One year in my writing boot camp, a talented writer presented her manuscript chapter to our group. Within minutes, interest shifted to boredom. Shoulders sagged. Yawns appeared. The verdict came swiftly: "Excellent ideas, lost in passive phrasing."

That night, reality hit me hard. I highlighted every "was" and "were" in my own manuscript. Yellow overwhelmed the pages. My powerful story—a narrative I knew intimately—felt flat on the page. I had created an unnecessary barrier between my story and my readers.

The Reader Experience

When you write in passive voice:

- Your readers disconnect
- They skim rather than absorb
- Their interest fades quickly
- The energy drops noticeably
- Connection breaks
- Impact disappears

Active Voice Creates Engagement

When you write in active voice:

- Your readers engage fully
- They experience immediacy
- They connect with action
- Energy intensifies
- Pace quickens
- Meaning sharpens

We read to experience, not to observe. Passive voice positions readers as distant observers. Active voice transforms them into participants.

Transformation Examples

Mystery:

- Passive: "The body was discovered by the detective near midnight."

- Active: "The detective discovered the body near midnight."

Romance:

- Passive: "Her heart was stolen by his unexpected kindness."

- Active: "His unexpected kindness stole her heart."

Fantasy:

- Passive: "The ancient spell was cast by the wizard, and the kingdom was plunged into darkness."

- Active: "The wizard cast the ancient spell, plunging the kingdom into darkness."

Literary Fiction:

- Passive: "The village was transformed by the arrival of the stranger."

- Active: "The stranger's arrival transformed the village."

The active versions pull you into the action rather than keeping you at a distance. They draw a direct line between cause and effect.

When Passive Voice Works

Despite its weaknesses, passive voice serves specific purposes in your books:

1. When the actor is unknown or irrelevant: "The mansion was constructed in 1887." (The builder's identity may be unknown or unimportant)

2. When you want to emphasize the recipient of action: "The children were rescued from the burning building." (Focus on the children, not rescuers)
3. To create mystery or suspense: "The letter was delivered at midnight." (Concealing who delivered it)
4. To maintain a character's limited perspective: "The shot was fired from somewhere in the darkness." (Character doesn't know who fired)

Here's a quick trick to identify passive voice: Add "by zombies" after the verb. If it makes sense, you've found passive voice:

- "The manuscript was written [by zombies]." ✓ PASSIVE
- "The author wrote the manuscript [by zombies]." ✗ ACTIVE

Fixing Passive Voice

- **Before:** "The town was terrorized by the serial killer."
- **After:** "The serial killer terrorized the town."

- **Before:** "The castle was surrounded by an army of thousands."
- **After:** "An army of thousands surrounded the castle."

- **Before:** "The story is told from multiple perspectives."

- **After:** "Multiple characters tell the story through their own perspectives."

Practice Exercise for Authors

Review your current manuscript chapter. Highlight every form of "to be" (am, is, are, was, were, being, been). Examine each instance. Can you replace it with a stronger, more direct construction? Challenge yourself to eliminate 80% of these passive constructions.

Active voice embraces accountability. It demonstrates confidence. It creates precision. It propels narrative. It captivates readers. It generates momentum. It conserves space. It magnifies impact.

The distinction between passive and active voice goes beyond grammar—it reveals your connection to authenticity. Passive voice watches life from a distance. Active voice lives within it. Passive voice records. Active voice speaks with conviction. Passive voice lists. Active voice engages.

Your stories deserve the strength of direct expression. They deserve the immediacy only active voice delivers. They deserve to breathe on the page rather than being preserved like specimens behind glass.

Keep your writing vibrant. Keep it active. Keep it moving.

Remember: great novelists don't eliminate passive voice entirely—they use it strategically and sparingly. Make conscious choices about when to employ each voice. Your readers will thank you with their undivided attention and emotional investment in your characters and worlds.

DO NOT MIX TENSES

The Time Contract: Why Tense Consistency Matters

Darrian walks into the kitchen. The morning sun had streamed through the window. She is making coffee when she noticed the note on the counter. Her hands start shaking as she had read the words.

Jarring, isn't it? Your brain just stumbled over a narrative obstacle course.

The Problem with Mixed Tenses

This is what happens when writers mix tenses. Readers' brains work overtime, mentally jumping between timeframes, struggling to orient themselves in the story's chronology.

My first professional editing job still haunts me. A promising thriller with strong characters and clever twists became nearly unreadable because of tense shifts. Present tense action scenes crashed into past tense dialogue. Characters thought in one timeframe and acted in another. The author had unknowingly created a temporal maze.

When I pointed this out, her response was devastating: "I didn't even notice." Three years of work, and she never realized she was constantly disorienting her readers.

Time is your story's invisible architecture. When it collapses, everything else falls.

Fixing Tense Inconsistency

Let's fix our example:

Present tense: Darrian walks into the kitchen. The morning sun streams through the window. She is making coffee when she notices the note on the counter. Her hands start shaking as she reads the words.

Past tense: Darrian walked into the kitchen. The morning sun streamed through the window. She was making coffee when she noticed the note on the counter. Her hands started shaking as she read the words.

The difference is immediate. The reader stays firmly anchored in one timeframe without having to recalibrate their mental timeline.

Common Tense-Mixing Errors

Writers who meticulously craft settings and characters often miss the temporal chaos they've created. It's like an artist obsessing over color while their canvas tears apart.

Common tense-mixing errors include:

Each inconsistency creates confusion. These moments accumulate, building a barrier between reader and story made of nothing but unnecessary cognitive effort.

The Rules of Tense

The rules are straightforward:

Present Tense creates immediacy for action happening now. Flashbacks use past tense. Future plans use will/going to. "I walk down the street. The sun shines bright. Tomorrow, I will meet her."

Past Tense provides perspective for completed action. Earlier events use past perfect (had). Future plans use would. "I walked down the street. The sun shone bright. Tomorrow, I would meet her."

When you switch incorrectly, readers lose their temporal bearings. Action becomes confusing. Immersion breaks. Flow stutters. Your credibility weakens.

One novelist couldn't understand why beta readers felt "seasick" reading her manuscript. The diagnosis: she unconsciously shifted from past to present tense during emotional scenes, trying to create immediacy but instead creating disorientation. Fixing this transformed her readers' experience.

Maintaining Consistent Tense

Choose your main tense and maintain it consistently across action sequences, dialogue, descriptions, thoughts, emotional moments, and transitions. This consistency forms the foundation your story builds upon.

Legitimate tense changes exist—clearly marked flashbacks, future plans in dialogue, chapters in different timelines, frame narratives. But these require clear signals, consistent patterns, and logical transitions to work.

Testing Your Tense Consistency

Test your writing by reading aloud. Mark every verb. They should align with your chosen tense unless you have a specific reason otherwise. Our ears often catch what our eyes miss—the awkward shift from "runs" to "had jumped" or "sang" to "is dancing."

Your readers need to understand when events happen, in what order, and how they relate. Without this clarity, even beautiful prose becomes a labyrinth.

The Time Contract

A developmental editor once told me: "Time is a contract between writer and reader." When you establish your tense, you're making a promise about how you'll navigate time. Breaking this promise without purpose weakens your readers' trust in you as their guide.

DO NOT MIX TENSES

Your story exists in time. Keep that time clear. Keep it consistent. Keep your readers grounded.

They should lose themselves in your story—not lose track of when it's happening.

DO NOT WRITE FAKE DIALOGUE

No one talks like this. Ever.

Yet writers keep creating dialogue that sounds like robots pretending to be human. Or worse—dialogue that exists solely to dump information on readers.

The Reality Check

In writing workshops, participants transcribe real conversations between people they know. The results always shock them—the fragments, interruptions, unfinished thoughts, verbal shortcuts between people sharing context. When compared with their fictional dialogue, one feels alive. The other feels manufactured.

Bad dialogue announces "amateur" from the first line.

Common Dialogue Killers

Information dumping: "As you know, Jim, since we've been married for twenty years..." No real person recites shared history like a Wikipedia entry. Try instead: "I can't believe Tommy's leaving for college already."

Name overuse: "Listen, Dianne, I need to tell you something, Dianne..." Count how often you use someone's name in actual conversation. Better: "Listen, I need to tell you something. This is important."

Perfect grammar: "I shall not be attending the function this evening..." Unless you're writing Victorian aristocrats, try: "Can't make it tonight. Something came up."

Explaining emotions: "I am crying because I am sad about our mother's death." Emotion needs no explanation when shown authentically: "I just... I miss Mom so much."

What Real Dialogue Does

Real dialogue has:

- Rhythm and energy
- Purpose in the story
- Distinctive character voices
- Conflict or tension
- Subtext beneath the surface
- Natural imperfections

People talk over each other. They leave thoughts unfinished. They use filler words—um, like, you know. They repeat themselves when anxious. They change subjects abruptly when uncomfortable. They misunderstand and talk past each other.

More Than Authenticity

Good dialogue:

- Reveals character
- Advances the plot
- Creates conflict
- Establishes relationships
- Conveys essential information naturally
- Breaks up descriptive sections
- Captures the book's tone

Feel the Difference

Unrealistic Romance: "My darling, my heart beats only for you, and I cannot imagine existing without your presence in my life."

Realistic Romance: "I just... God, I can't imagine doing this without you." "Hey. You don't have to."

Unrealistic Conflict: "I am extremely angry with you because you failed to complete the tasks I assigned!"

Realistic Conflict: "You had one job." "I know, okay? I know. I messed up."

The difference isn't just in length—it's in emotional depth. Real people don't always express their feelings with perfect clarity. They stumble toward meaning. They mask vulnerability with anger. They say simple things that carry complex emotions.

Making Dialogue Real

With every line, consider who's speaking and to whom. What's their relationship? What's the situation? What remains unsaid? What does each person want? What might they be hiding?

The Power of Less

In dialogue, less is often more. Subtext holds more weight than the words themselves. Actions complement words. Silence speaks volumes. Natural flow outweighs grammatical perfection. Character shapes expression. Authenticity resonates with readers.

Listen to real conversations around you. Notice interruptions, unfinished thoughts, topic changes, inside jokes, and uncomfortable pauses.

Your dialogue needs to sound like people talking—not characters reciting lines. It should feel alive, unpredictable, flawed, and authentic.

Because readers know how people talk.

They live it every day.

DO NOT SWITCH VIEWPOINTS RANDOMLY

Point of View: Your Story's Camera Lens

She opened the door. I couldn't believe what I was seeing. You might think this wouldn't matter, but we all knew differently. He had been there the whole time.

Feel that mental whiplash? That's what happens when point of view ricochets through your prose. Every POV shift yanks readers out of your story, forcing them to recalibrate whose perspective they're experiencing.

A thriller manuscript taught me this lesson permanently. The story—compelling at its core with a missing child, desperate mother, and secretive town—began in close third person, slipped into first for a paragraph, wandered into second for a reflection, then somehow ended with omniscient narration. Despite the gripping premise, I couldn't emotionally commit because I kept being thrown from one perspective to another.

When confronted, the author seemed genuinely confused: "But these are all valid perspectives. I'm using the right voice for each moment."

Here's what the author missed: Point of view isn't about technical correctness—it's about reader connection. Each shift creates distance. Each jump breaks immersion. Each change forces readers to rebuild their relationship with your narrative.

Think of POV as a contract with your reader about how they'll experience your story. Breaking that contract feels like betrayal, however subtle.

Your POV Options

First Person ("I")

Puts readers directly behind a character's eyes: I walked into the room. I saw the letter. I couldn't believe it.

Strengths:

- Creates immediate intimacy with the character
- Provides direct access to inner thoughts
- Builds stronger emotional connection
- Works well for character-driven stories
- Limits information to what the character knows

Limitations:

- Restricts perspective to one character's knowledge
- Can't show what happens outside character's presence
- Biases all information through single perspective

- Makes revealing character flaws more challenging
- Can feel too personal for some readers

Second Person ("You")

Casts the reader as a participant: You walk into the room. You see the letter. You can't believe it.

Strengths:

- Creates unique immediacy and involvement
- Works powerfully for instructional content
- Pulls readers directly into the story
- Effective for certain interactive genres
- Creates distinctive voice

Limitations:

- Quickly becomes exhausting for readers
- Creates resistance if readers don't identify with actions
- Difficult to sustain for longer works
- Better for short pieces or experimental fiction
- Can feel gimmicky if not expertly handled

Third Person Limited ("He/She/They")

Offers flexibility while maintaining focus: She walked into the room. She saw the letter. She couldn't believe it.

Strengths:

- Balances intimacy with narrative distance
- Allows deeper character development than omniscient
- Can move between characters (between scenes/chapters)
- Provides objective description with subjective experience
- Most versatile and widely used in contemporary fiction

Limitations:

- Requires careful handling when shifting between characters
- Must maintain consistent narrative distance
- Can't show what the focused character doesn't perceive
- Requires skill to reveal character flaws naturally
- May feel less immediate than first person

Third Person Omniscient

Provides the broadest lens: La'Shon walked in, wondering what Eric was thinking. Eric watched her, knowing he had to tell her soon.

Strengths:

- Shows multiple perspectives simultaneously

- Provides context beyond any character's knowledge
- Creates broader scope and epic feel
- Allows commentary on characters and events
- Gives freedom to reveal any information

Limitations:

- Creates emotional distance from characters
- More difficult to establish deep character connection
- Requires skilled handling to avoid head-hopping
- Can feel old-fashioned to contemporary readers
- Makes maintaining tension more challenging

Common POV Mistakes

Head-hopping: Jumping between characters' minds without warning.

- Problem: Creates confusion about whose thoughts/feelings we're experiencing
- Fix: Maintain one perspective per scene or use clear transitions

Inconsistent Distance: Shifting narrative distance illogically.

- Problem: Readers can't settle into consistent relationship with narrator
- Fix: Decide on narrative distance and maintain it consistently

Confused Perspective: Limited perspective showing what it couldn't know.

- Problem: Breaks reader trust by violating established POV rules
- Fix: Only reveal what your chosen POV character could reasonably know

---

Choose your POV based on:

- Whose story it is fundamentally
- What emotional connection you want readers to feel
- What information must be revealed or concealed
- The scope and scale of your narrative
- Genre expectations and conventions

That thriller manuscript? After revision with consistent third-person limited perspective—shifting only between chapters with clear focus on one character at a time—the transformation was stunning. Without changing the core story, the author created an immersive experience where before there had been constant disruption.

Remember: POV is your camera, filter, voice, guide, and contract with readers about how they'll experience your fictional world.

Test your POV by asking:

- Who has the most at stake in this story?

DO NOT SWITCH VIEWPOINTS RANDOMLY

- What perspective best reveals the heart of the conflict?
- What information do I need to conceal or reveal?
- How close do I want readers to feel to my characters?
- What are readers of my genre accustomed to?

Your POV choice shapes everything—from setting descriptions to information reveals, emotional impact to action pacing, tension building to revelation timing.

Choose with purpose. Maintain with care. Switch with skill.

Because your readers need to trust where you're leading them—and how you're showing them the view.

DO NOT INFO-DUMP

When Information Overload Kills Your Story

Mocha Brown stood 6'2" tall with brown hair and green eyes. Born in Seattle in 1992. Washington State University graduate, criminal justice degree. Five years as a police officer, now a private investigator. Divorced. Lives with golden retriever Max. Trust issues from ex-wife cheating with his former partner.

Close this book yet?

That's exactly what readers do when you dump a character's entire biography in their laps. Or when you start with three pages explaining your fantasy world's political system. Or when you open with a quantum physics lecture to set up your sci-fi premise.

Information dumping drowns readers in a flood of details they never asked for. They choke on facts without emotional context, gasping for story while you pump more information into their lungs.

We do this from fear. Fear readers won't understand our world without exhaustive explanation. Fear they'll miss our carefully crafted character histories. Fear they'll abandon the book without grasping every nuance. This fear creates exactly what we dread—giving them reason to stop reading.

When was the last time you met someone at a party and immediately wanted their complete life history, educational background, and psychological profile? Information earns its place through connection. We want to know more about people once they've intrigued us, not before.

Information should be:

- Relevant to the moment
- Natural to the scene
- Important to current action
- Woven into story flow
- Connected to character experience
- Delivered when needed—not before

Each genre carries its own information burden, but delivery principles remain universal.

The temptation to explain overwhelms many speculative fiction writers. We've built entire worlds—political systems, magic rules, technology frameworks, alien societies. But forcing this all at once feels like mandatory tourism rather than discovery.

DO NOT INFO-DUMP

Compare:

BAD: "The Mages of Alaria wielded elemental magic through crystal focuses, mined from the Northern Mountains during the Third Age after the Great War between the Five Kingdoms..."

BETTER: "The crystal cracked in Maya's grip, its power fading. Of course the black market dealer had sold her a fake—real Alarian crystals hadn't been mined since the kingdoms fell."

The first drowns us in history without context. The second shows a present problem hinting at history—a character facing consequences that reveal world rules.

- Failed magic reveals system limits
- Broken technology shows advancement level
- Cultural conflicts expose social structures
- Resource scarcity hints at history
- Character struggles illuminate world rules

Mystery and Thriller: Expertise Through Action

Detective backgrounds, case histories, forensic procedures—these should emerge through action, not resume recitation.

BAD: "Detective Michelle Chavis had solved fifteen homicides in her ten-year career, earning commendations for..."

BETTER: "Michelle's commendation wall blurred as she

stared at the crime scene photos. Sixteen solved homicides, and none like this."

- Investigation reveals background
- Partner dialogue shows experience
- Crime scene reactions show expertise
- Procedural choices show training
- Professional conflicts show reputation

Romance: Show the Walls Before Explaining Them

Romance writers often front-load relationship histories and physical descriptions, telling why characters fear love before showing them in action.

BAD: "After her last three relationships ended badly, Eila had given up on dating, focusing instead on her career as a pediatric surgeon..."

BETTER: "Eila's phone buzzed with another dating app notification. She swiped delete without looking, her surgeon's hands steady even after twelve hours in the OR."

Show relationship readiness through current interactions, daily choices, friend conversations, work-life balance, and small decisions. Let us see the walls before explaining why they were built.

Literary Fiction: Revelation Through Action

Family histories and character psychologies deserve revelation through action, not explanation.

BAD: "The Smith family had lived in the small town for four generations, carrying the weight of their ancestors' choices..."

BETTER: "Ryder touched the crack in the family portrait's frame, the same crack his grandmother had touched every Sunday for forty years."

Layer meaning through symbolic objects, routine actions, generational patterns, environmental details, and repeated moments. Trust readers to assemble the puzzle if you provide the pieces.

Historical Fiction: Context Through Conflict

Historical fiction requires context, but not as textbook introduction.

BAD: "In 1842, London's social season followed strict protocols, with young ladies of good breeding..."

BETTER: "Roman's gloves had a spot of ink—social suicide in 1842 London, but he'd rather read than be proper."

Show historical context through character restrictions, social conflicts, personal choices, daily challenges, and cultural clashes. Let the past live through present action.

Even Non-Fiction Benefits from Showing Before Telling

Methods and theories gain power through example and application, not abstract explanation.

BAD: "The psychological principles of behavior change were established through decades of research..."

BETTER: "Imagine trying to eat an elephant. Impossible, right? Now imagine eating it one bite at a time. That's how lasting change happens."

Build understanding through relatable examples, reader exercises, progressive steps, personal stories, and practical applications. Meet your readers where they live before asking them to follow you elsewhere.

When I revised my biographical disaster of a first chapter, I started with my character picking a lock in pouring rain. His expertise revealed background. His worn wedding ring hinted at loss. His conversation with his dog suggested loneliness. His methodical approach showed training. By the time readers learned he was ex-police, they already cared about why he'd left the force.

Your readers aren't here to study—they're here to experience. Give them reason to want information before providing it. Let them discover your world one natural detail at a time.

Information doesn't create connection—connection creates desire for information. Make them curious first. Make them care.

DO NOT NEGLECT CHARACTER DEVELOPMENT

No one talks like this. Ever.

Yet writers keep creating dialogue that sounds like robots pretending to be human. Or worse—dialogue that exists solely to dump information on readers.

The Reality Check

In writing workshops, participants transcribe real conversations between people they know. The results always shock them—the fragments, interruptions, unfinished thoughts, verbal shortcuts between people sharing context. When compared with their fictional dialogue, one feels alive. The other feels manufactured.

Bad dialogue announces "amateur" from the first line.

Common Dialogue Killers

Information dumping: "As you know, Jim, since we've been married for twenty years..." No real person recites shared history like a Wikipedia entry. Try instead: "I can't believe Tommy's leaving for college already."

Name overuse: "Listen, Dianne, I need to tell you something, Dianne..." Count how often you use someone's name in actual conversation. Better: "Listen, I need to tell you something. This is important."

Perfect grammar: "I shall not be attending the function this evening..." Unless you're writing Victorian aristocrats, try: "Can't make it tonight. Something came up."

Explaining emotions: "I am crying because I am sad about our mother's death." Emotion needs no explanation when shown authentically: "I just... I miss Mom so much."

What Real Dialogue Does

Real dialogue has:

- Rhythm and energy
- Purpose in the story
- Distinctive character voices
- Conflict or tension
- Subtext beneath the surface
- Natural imperfections

People talk over each other. They leave thoughts unfinished. They use filler words—um, like, you know. They repeat themselves when anxious. They change subjects abruptly when uncomfortable. They misunderstand and talk past each other.

More Than Authenticity

Good dialogue:

- Reveals character
- Advances the plot
- Creates conflict
- Establishes relationships
- Conveys essential information naturally
- Breaks up descriptive sections
- Captures the book's tone

Feel the Difference

Unrealistic Romance: "My darling, my heart beats only for you, and I cannot imagine existing without your presence in my life."

Realistic Romance: "I just... God, I can't imagine doing this without you." "Hey. You don't have to."

Unrealistic Conflict: "I am extremely angry with you because you failed to complete the tasks I assigned!"

Realistic Conflict: "You had one job." "I know, okay? I know. I messed up."

The difference isn't just in length—it's in emotional depth. Real people don't always express their feelings with perfect clarity. They stumble toward meaning. They mask vulnerability with anger. They say simple things that carry complex emotions.

Making Dialogue Real

With every line, consider who's speaking and to whom. What's their relationship? What's the situation? What remains unsaid? What does each person want? What might they be hiding?

Four Powerful Character Development Exercises

To create characters who speak authentically, you need to know them deeply. These exercises will help you discover the foundations that make dialogue ring true:

1. The Pressure Test

Discover your character's core by breaking them: Put your character in a situation of extreme pressure or crisis. When everything is stripped away, what remains? What lines will they never cross? What unexpected strengths emerge?

Characters reveal their true nature under extreme pressure. This exercise often uncovers depths you hadn't consciously developed.

2. The Supporting Character Promotion

Temporarily make a secondary character your protagonist: Write a pivotal scene from your story from a supporting character's perspective. What motivations and judgments emerge that you hadn't considered?

This exercise prevents secondary characters from becoming plot devices or stereotypes.

3. The Value Hierarchy Ranking

Determine what matters most to your character: Create a ranked list of values your character holds dear (family, ambition, loyalty, etc.). Force yourself to put them in strict order of importance.

This hierarchy will guide authentic choices throughout your narrative.

4. The Wound Excavation

Develop the formative experiences that shaped your character: What past hurt or disappointment most influences your character's current behavior? How old were they? Who was involved?

You don't need to include this scene in your story, but knowing it will inform every aspect of your character's behavior.

The Power of Less

In dialogue, less is often more. Subtext holds more weight than the words themselves. Actions complement words. Silence speaks volumes. Natural flow outweighs grammatical perfection. Character shapes expression. Authenticity resonates with readers.

Listen to real conversations around you. Notice interruptions, unfinished thoughts, topic changes, inside jokes, and uncomfortable pauses.

Your dialogue needs to sound like people talking—not characters reciting lines. It should feel alive, unpredictable, flawed, and authentic.

Because readers know how people talk.

They live it every day.

DO NOT START SLOWLY

I attended a writing class at a college (before attending Full Sail) renowned for producing successful writers. The award-winning professor gave me a C because I started my book with drama. When I asked for an example of how it should start, the professor said, "slow."

Don't you do that. Something needs to capture that reader. That opening line is everything.

Think about this - Your book sits on a shelf surrounded by countless others. A potential reader picks it up and flips through the first few pages. You have thirty seconds—probably less—to make them care.

They read:

"The morning dawned clear and bright. Birds chirped in the trees as Easton woke up and stretched. He got out of bed,

walked to the bathroom, brushed his teeth, and started getting ready for what would be an interesting day..."

The book returns to the shelf, unread.

Another reader picks up a different book:

I walk into the dead woman's office expecting to find a suicide note. What I find instead is a confession.

The kind written in frantic, almost violent strokes across the wall behind her desk. Words only visible now because of the blacklight the detective accidentally triggered when leaning against the switch.

"I didn't kill him. I made him kill himself."

This book goes home with the reader.

The difference is clear: one opening creates questions. The other creates boredom.

Your opening carries the promise of your entire book. It tells readers, "This matters. Stick with me. I'll make you feel something."

A weak opening suggests, "Maybe it gets better later." But most of today's readers won't wait for "later." They demand to feel something immediately.

Consider how stories spread in real life: "You won't believe what happened today..." "I have to tell you the craziest thing..." We start with what burns, what grabs attention, what forces the listener to ask, "What happened next?"

Your story deserves that same respect. Start where the energy is. Where the question burns. Where the heart catches.

Effective openings across genres:

- **Thriller:** "The night I killed my father, the moon was full."
- **Romance:** "Annabeth knew the exact moment she'd fall in love. This wasn't it."
- **Literary:** "The boy was born with a hole where his heart should have been."
- **Fantasy:** "The dragon's shadow passed over the village for the third time that week—always on market day, always at noon."

Each makes readers ask questions and want to know more. They pull readers in and promise something worth their time.

Your hook must:

- Create questions
- Establish voice
- Suggest conflict
- Hint at stakes
- Promise a journey worth taking

Avoid:

- Weather reports
- Morning routines
- Character descriptions

- Backstory dumps
- Dreams (unless crucial)
- Excessive worldbuilding

Your opening should grab readers like a firm, purposeful handshake—confident in its direction.

Ask yourself:

• What's the most interesting moment in my story?

• What's the first point of no return for my character?

• What question would make ME keep reading?

• What emotion do I want readers to feel first?

Don't provide immediate answers. Make the questions come first.

The perfect moment to start your story likely exists within your draft already—often not on your first page. It might be in Chapter Two, Three, or halfway through your manuscript.

Find that moment. Start there.

Everything else becomes flashbacks. Gradual revelations. Crafted hints.

Trust your readers to follow you into the unknown, but first, make them want to. Give them a reason. A hook. A promise worth keeping.

In a world of endless distractions, "it gets better later" is no longer enough.

DO NOT AVOID EMOTIONAL DEPTH

Emotional depth isn't just decorative—it's the lifeblood of memorable writing. When a character experiences loss, "Jasmine felt sad" tells us nothing. It's a label, not an experience.

Instead, show us this:

Jasmine traced her fingers along bare walls with empty nail holes like wounds in the plaster. Their wedding photo had hung there. She tilted her head to avoid seeing her ghost-like reflection in the window. Behind her, John's inherited grandfather clock marked empty minutes, its tick-tock filling the space his voice once occupied.

That's the difference.

The Power of Showing, Not Telling

Real emotional depth means inhabiting feelings, not naming them. It creates moments so authentic readers forget they're reading—they're too busy experiencing the raw emotion alongside the characters.

Writers constantly fall into lazy shortcuts: "He was angry." "She felt nervous." "They were in love." These aren't emotions but labels that point toward feelings without making readers feel anything.

Sources of Authentic Emotional Depth

Authentic emotional depth emerges from:

Physical manifestations: His knuckles whitened against the steering wheel as traffic crawled past the hospital entrance. Minutes ticking by when the doctor had warned, "If treatment doesn't start exactly on schedule..."

Environmental cues: The kitchen still smelled like her mother's coffee, the unwashed mug leaving a perfect ring on the counter. Three weeks after the funeral, that small circle remained—stale but sacred.

Psychological complexity: Each word in her email felt like betrayal. Professional. Distant. Perfect. No reader would guess she'd carried his child or still reached for him at 3 a.m.

The Courage to Go Deeper

This depth requires courage to:

DO NOT AVOID EMOTIONAL DEPTH

- Confront your own emotional truths
- Write beyond comfortable boundaries
- Trust readers to understand nuance
- Avoid the safety of familiar tropes
- Resist explaining what should be felt

Strong vs. Weak Emotional Writing

Consider these contrasts:

Weak: "Reggie was nervous about seeing his father again."

Strong: The diner looked unchanged—cracked vinyl booths, coffee-stained menus, cigarette burns on the countertop. Reggie chose the farthest booth, where flickering lights blurred reality's edges. Fifteen years collapsed between heartbeats. He straightened his collar, smoothed his hair—the boy still trying to prevent inevitable criticism.

Weak: "Dianne missed her sister."

Strong: Dianne kept Shirley's last voicemail, though she hadn't played it in months. "Hey, just checking in..." Words with no hint of what was coming. Her finger often hovered over play but never pressed it. As long as she didn't listen, her sister was still just checking in, still about to finish their forever-interrupted conversation.

Building Psychological Tension

Psychological tension builds through:

- Conflicting desires within characters

- Unspoken subtext in dialogue
- Gaps between perception and reality
- Moments that force impossible choices
- Small gestures that reveal deeper truths

Creating Complex Characters

Characters need to:

- Harbor conflicting desires
- Face internal obstacles
- Carry unresolved wounds
- Make imperfect decisions
- Operate from mixed motives

Embracing Emotional Contradictions

Human emotion is never simple—it's layered and contradictory:

- We can feel love and resentment toward the same person
- Relief can mix with guilt
- Hope often contains fear
- Pride intertwines with shame
- Longing can exist alongside contentment

Honoring Complexity in Stories

A story must honor this complexity by allowing characters to:

- Make decisions that surprise even themselves
- Experience conflicting emotions simultaneously
- Hold inconsistent beliefs
- Act against their own interests at times
- Change through the story's events, often reluctantly

Finding Clarity in the Spaces

Clarity lives between what we show and what we hide. Between words and meaning. Between identity and pretense.

Find those spaces. Inhabit them. Let readers navigate through the darkness until they discover their own insights reflected in your words.

That's what stories are—lights in the dark, helping us feel less alone with our most human complexities.

DO NOT END WITHOUT RESOLUTION

The last page turns. The book closes. In that silence between final word and reality's return, your reader sits with what you've given them. What remains determines whether your book lives in their heart or dies in their memory.

An unsatisfying ending betrays every promise you've made. Every hour invested. Every emotional connection formed. Every question carried through sleepless nights.

Readers throw books across rooms, faces twisted in betrayal. Not because the ending was sad or happy, but because it wasn't an ending at all. Just a stop. A surrender. An abandonment.

Your readers deserve better.

Understanding Endings

It's like a relationship ending—there's a difference between a careful goodbye and someone simply walking away. Readers need that goodbye. They need closure. They need to know their investment mattered.

Readers should feel both satisfied and hungry—satisfied that this part mattered, hungry for where the larger journey leads.

Beware false cliffhangers. Ending mid-scene isn't tension—it's manipulation. Even series books need emotional completion.

Types of Endings

The Full Circle: Returns to where we began, but everything has changed
The Epilogue: Shows characters after the dust settles
The Open Door: Resolves the main conflict while hinting at future possibilities
The Twist: Reframes everything that came before
The Inevitable: Delivers exactly what must happen, even if painful
The Revelation: Unveils a final truth that changes everything

Common Resolution Mistakes

- **Deus ex machina:** Problems solved by convenient coincidence
- **Character betrayal:** Actions inconsistent with established traits
- **Too tidy:** Every loose end wrapped up artificially

- **Abandoned threads:** Major questions left completely unanswered
- **Rushed closure:** Complex issues resolved too quickly
- **Extended epilogue:** Dragging beyond natural ending point

For Series Writers

- Each book needs its own emotional resolution
- Primary story questions can continue, but each volume needs satisfying closure
- Character growth must occur in every book
- Cliffhangers should involve new questions, not unresolved main conflicts
- Readers should feel rewarded for finishing, not frustrated

Your Resolution Checklist

- Does it fulfill the promise of your premise?
- Has your protagonist completed a meaningful arc?
- Are the story's central questions addressed?
- Does it reflect your book's theme?
- Is the emotional tone consistent with your story?
- Would a reader recommend this book based on its ending?
- Does it feel both surprising and inevitable?

Your ending is a lens focusing every element into a single, powerful point of light. It should illuminate everything that came before while burning itself into memory.

Readers forgive many things—slow starts, saggy middles, minor inconsistencies. But they never forget a betrayed ending.

Give them the ending they need, even if it's not expected.

Ensure it's deserved. Guarantee it resonates. Confirm it has significance.

Because in that silence after the last page turns, your story either lives forever or dies completely.

Make it live.

DO NOT IGNORE EMOTIONAL STAKES

A thrilling plot packed with twists and action keeps pages turning, but without emotional connection, readers won't care. Period. Stories aren't just event sequences—they're experiences that matter to actual human beings.

The Problem of Emotionally Hollow Stories

Many manuscripts have everything a thriller needs—car chases, explosions, clever twists—yet leave readers feeling absolutely nothing after the final page. The plot functions like a well-oiled machine, but the protagonist remains a stranger through hundreds of pages of adventure.

The crucial question for any story: "Why should readers care if your hero lives or dies?"

Without emotional stakes, books become mere event sequences, not experiences. Readers might enjoy the moment but forget everything five minutes after closing the book. The stories that stay with us don't just stimulate thought—they gut-punch us with feeling.

Signs Your Story Lacks Emotional Depth

The solution isn't adding more danger, action, or plot twists. It's adding meaning.

How to Build Emotional Stakes

1. Create Personal Consequences

Give your character something deeply personal to lose beyond the external conflict. In "The Hunger Games," Katniss isn't just fighting for survival—she's protecting her sister Prim. This emotional connection intensifies every moment in the Games. Her volunteering as tribute isn't mere plot advancement—it's an emotional cornerstone that anchors the entire story.

2. Force Difficult Choices

Every significant decision should carry emotional weight. If your protagonist moves forward without internal struggle, stakes feel artificial. In "The Fault in Our Stars," Hazel's relationship with Augustus isn't just romance—it's deciding whether love justifies inevitable grief. Every happy moment carries future pain's shadow, creating emotional tension that makes their story unforgettable.

3. Link External Conflict to Internal Growth

The hero's journey must be psychological and emotional, not just physical. Obstacles should transform characters, not just challenge them. In "A Christmas Carol," Scrooge's supernatural journey directly parallels his evolution from bitterness to compassion. The ghosts aren't plot devices—they're mirrors forcing him to confront his humanity. His Christmas morning joy resonates because readers have experienced his complete transformation.

4. Create Emotionally Satisfying Resolutions

Readers need more than solved mysteries or defeated villains—outcomes must mean something. In "Avengers: Endgame," Tony Stark's sacrifice completes his journey from selfish playboy to selfless hero. His death resonates because it represents the culmination of profound personal growth. The plot and emotional resolutions converge, creating genuine catharsis.

The Lasting Impact of Emotional Investment

Plot without emotion is just movement—clever sequences that readers quickly forget. Give your characters personal stakes. Make choices cost something meaningful. Connect external journeys to internal growth. Ensure resolutions satisfy emotionally, not just logically.

Readers need investment in outcomes, not just awareness of them. The most memorable plots aren't about action alone—they're about transformation. If your story doesn't evoke emotion, it won't endure in memory.

Add emotional stakes, and your story will resonate long after readers turn the final page.

DO NOT ADD POINTLESS SUBPLOTS

The Critical Role of Subplots

A novel with only one plot thread—like a protagonist's search for a missing artifact—may seem focused, but it's actually incomplete. Without subplots, a story isn't streamlined—it's skeletal. Life doesn't happen in a single dimension. Neither should your story.

A manuscript with only one plot thread reads like a video game walkthrough rather than a living world. The protagonist exists in a vacuum where nothing matters except the main conflict. The story moves forward but never expands outward.

The Subplot Balancing Act

Strong subplots add depth, complexity, and emotional weight. Weak ones derail your entire story.

A mystery novel with seven subplots—each fascinating individually but collectively overwhelming—can swallow the main murder investigation. By chapter ten, readers can't remember who was murdered, let alone care about solving the crime. The subplots become a tangled forest where the main path vanishes completely.

Here's your non-negotiable rule: If your subplot doesn't serve a purpose, cut it. Today.

Connect everything to the main story. In "The Hunger Games," Peeta's romance subplot isn't just about love—it directly impacts Katniss's survival strategy, raises the stakes, and influences how the Capitol perceives her. Suzanne Collins didn't take a detour from the hunger games—she complicated them meaningfully.

Develop characters through subplots. In "Pride and Prejudice," Charlotte Lucas's marriage to Mr. Collins isn't random—it reveals Elizabeth's core values and what she refuses to compromise on. This subplot deepens our understanding of Elizabeth while reinforcing the novel's themes about marriage and social expectations.

Maintain balance. In Harry Potter, the Marauder's Map subplot gives Harry tools to investigate but doesn't overshadow his confrontation with Sirius Black. It serves the main story while adding world-building and connecting Harry to his father.

Resolve everything with purpose. In "Breaking Bad," Hank's investigation subplot doesn't just disappear—it builds tension and ultimately creates a major turning point. Its resolution directly impacts the primary conflict.

Transformation Through Intentional Subplots

A contemporary fiction manuscript can be transformed by reimagining its subplots. Consider a draft containing a workplace rivalry, home renovation, and sick parent storyline alongside the main narrative about post-divorce rebuilding.

The workplace rivalry might develop the protagonist's confidence and the renovation could perfectly symbolize rebuilding a life. But if the sick parent subplot exists in isolation, it becomes problematic.

Rather than cutting it, finding connections helps—how caregiving forces the protagonist to confront vulnerability, how family obligations complicate independence, how witnessing mortality shifts perspective on divorce. Suddenly, this subplot isn't a distraction but a meaningful counterpoint.

Subplots as Series Foundations

Well-crafted subplots can become the foundation for an entire series. When strategically developed, they can:

J.K. Rowling planted numerous subplots in early Harry Potter books (the Marauders' backstory, Voldemort's history) that later became central to the series. George R.R. Martin's "A Song of Ice and Fire" contains countless subplots that expand the world and create material for multiple books.

The key is ensuring these subplots feel purposeful in the original book (not just obvious sequel bait), enhance rather than distract from the main story, create genuine reader curiosity, and contain enough depth to sustain expanded exploration.

Subplots should add depth, not drag your story off course. Well-crafted subplots make your narrative feel real, complex, and unforgettable. They don't need equal weight, but they do need purpose.

Tighten your subplots. Your book will emerge stronger, richer, more immersive—and potentially the beginning of something much bigger.

DO NOT EXPLAIN EVERYTHING

Show, Don't Tell: The Difference Between Information and Experience

I wrestled with this principle for what felt like forever. I honestly believed I had a handle on it because I'd already published a novel with my mentor and been part of 4 separate anthologies. I was pumped to tackle my first solo manuscript. Fast forward 4 months—I had this swollen 80,000+ word beast where I basically explained everything outright. If I'd actually mastered the art of showing rather than telling, that one book would've naturally expanded into three. Complete disaster. It was garbage.

When my mentor read out loud: "Madison was afraid of commitment because her father had abandoned the family when she was seven," then challenged me to show instead of tell, I didn't get it. Hadn't I made myself clear? Wasn't that crucial background?

"Yes," my mentor responded, "but understanding something isn't experiencing it. You've delivered facts, not feelings."

That insight completely revolutionized my approach to writing.

The Core Principle

Powerful storytelling isn't about transferring information—it's about creating total immersion. Readers don't want a report of events; they want to experience them firsthand.

How to Transform Telling into Showing

Use Physical Details to Convey Emotion

Instead of: "She was furious when she saw him with another woman."

Write: "Her jaw clenched, fingers tightening around her glass. The ice cracked as she took a slow, measured breath."

The second version never names the emotion, yet you feel it more intensely through specific physical detail.

Reveal Information Through Natural Interaction

Instead of: "Chris had been a cop for ten years, but ever since his wife left, he drank too much."

Write: "Chris tossed his badge onto the bar and downed another whiskey. 'Ten years of chasing criminals, and I still couldn't hold onto the one thing that mattered.'"

Same information, but delivered through a lived moment rather than an author's explanation.

Let Setting Create Atmosphere

Instead of: "The abandoned house was creepy and run-down, with broken windows and creaky floors."

Write: "The wind rattled a loose shutter against the siding. Dust coated the windows, filtering the moonlight into ghostly streaks. The wooden floor groaned under every cautious step."

Specific sensory details create emotional impact beyond what simple description can achieve.

Release Backstory Gradually

Instead of: "She had grown up in foster care, moving from home to home, never knowing stability."

Write: "She hesitated before knocking, gripping her bag tighter. Homes never lasted, but she still clung to the hope that maybe, this time, things would be different."

The second approach hints at history while keeping readers engaged in the present moment.

Use All Five Senses

Don't limit your descriptions to just what characters see. Incorporate sound, smell, taste, and touch to create a fully immersive experience that pulls readers into the scene.

Balance Showing with Efficient Telling

Not everything needs to be shown. Sometimes a direct statement serves the story better, particularly for transitions or minor details. The key is knowing when to expand through showing and when to compress through telling.

After that workshop revelation, I rewrote my scene about Madison. I showed her slipping out of her boyfriend's apartment at 2 a.m., carefully extracting herself from his embrace. I revealed her ritual of maintaining her own apartment despite sleeping at his place most nights. When her boyfriend suggested moving in together, I showed her freezing, suddenly seeing her father's face the morning he packed his car. I depicted her compulsively checking her phone when someone was late, her rising panic, her flood of relief when they appeared.

I never wrote "Madison had commitment issues from childhood abandonment." I didn't need to. Readers felt it through her actions, understood it through carefully placed flashbacks, and experienced her struggle emotionally rather than processing it intellectually.

Your goal as a writer isn't to explain—it's to evoke. Make readers feel, not just read. Show emotions, history, and world-building through action, dialogue, and sensory details.

Cut unnecessary explanations. Your book will immediately feel more immersive, cinematic, and compelling.

III. EDITING & REVISION MISTAKES

DO NOT IGNORE BETA READER FEEDBACK

The email sits unopened in the inbox, a beta reader's feedback waiting like a held breath. The cursor hovers over it, trembling slightly. Inside these unread words lies a stranger's first encounter with the story—a heart bound in digital pages, waiting for judgment.

The Beta Reader Relationship

Stories don't live in writers' minds. They live in the space between writer and reader, in that delicate transfer of imagination and emotion that happens when someone else's eyes trace the words on the page.

Beta readers inhabit that space. They stand where future readers will stand, experiencing the story with fresh eyes and unmarked hearts. They see what's really there, not what the author meant to put there.

What Beta Readers Provide

Beta readers catch what authors can't:

- Plot holes invisible to creators too close to their work
- Character inconsistencies that break reader trust
- Pacing issues that cause engagement to falter
- Confusing passages that seem clear to the author
- Emotional impact (or lack thereof) of key scenes
- Unintended implications or messages

They show authors where the story lives and where it dies, where it soars and where it stumbles, where it reveals itself and where it hides behind pretense.

Choosing the Right Beta Readers

Not all beta readers are created equal. The best approach is to assemble a diverse team:

- Genre readers who understand conventions and expectations
- Non-genre readers who spot issues hidden by familiarity
- Detail-oriented readers who catch inconsistencies
- Emotionally intuitive readers who track character arcs
- Industry professionals who understand market realities
- Target demographic readers who represent your audience

Avoid choosing only friends and family who may hesitate to provide honest criticism. Not all feedback carries equal weight.

When to Ignore Feedback

Authors should trust their vision when:

- Feedback contradicts the core premise or theme
- Suggestions would fundamentally change the story's identity
- Multiple readers disagree about the same element
- Criticism focuses on personal preference rather than craft
- Feedback asks for a different book entirely
- Their writer's instinct strongly objects (after careful consideration)

Common Beta Reader Feedback Pitfalls

Many authors make critical mistakes with beta reader feedback:

- Defending their choices instead of listening
- Implementing every suggestion without discrimination
- Explaining what they "meant" instead of fixing clarity issues
- Taking criticism personally rather than professionally
- Asking loaded questions that fish for praise
- Dismissing consistent feedback from multiple readers

- Failing to distinguish between subjective opinions and objective craft issues

The Feedback-Revision Cycle

For maximum benefit, consider:

- Providing specific questions alongside general impressions
- Using multiple rounds with different readers
- Taking time between receiving feedback and revising
- Tracking patterns across different readers' responses
- Addressing fundamental issues before line-level concerns
- Being clear about what stage the manuscript is in
- Expressing gratitude regardless of how critical the feedback

Beta readers aren't enemies or critics. They're allies in bringing the story to life. They stand in for the thousands of readers who will one day hold the book, turning pages, hoping to find something that matters.

They offer authors a precious gift: The chance to see the story through new eyes. To understand its impact on hearts they don't know. To bridge the gap between vision and readers' experience.

That gift shouldn't be wasted. Their confusion shouldn't be dismissed. Their questions shouldn't be explained away.

Author choices shouldn't be defended before considering their impact.

Every story deserves readers who can see it clearly.

DO NOT SKIP PROFESSIONAL EDITING OR DISMISS FEEDBACK

The Editor - Writer Relationship: Your Book's Success Depends On It

The manuscript sits before you, every word gleaming with perfection. You've read it so many times you can recite whole passages from memory. Each sentence feels carved from your heart, each paragraph polished by your devotion.

The very thought of someone else touching your words makes your chest tight. This is the moment where careers die. Where beautiful books become missed opportunities. Where years of work crumble into "almost made it."

Then, when you do finally invest in professional editing, the manuscript returns covered in red ink - chapters crossed out, beloved scenes marked for deletion, cherished characters flagged for removal. Your chest tightens. Your hands shake. This feels like butchery, not editing.

Both reactions come from the same dangerous misconception: that your book belongs to you alone. In reality, your book exists in the space between writer and reader, and only professional editing can bridge that gap effectively.

The Gap Between Intention and Reality

The story in your head isn't the one on the page. The emotions you feel reading your work aren't what readers will experience. The clarity you think exists simply isn't there for anyone but you.

I learned this the hard way with my first self-help manuscript. For six months, I'd poured every insight from ten years of experience into what I believed was revolutionary material. I convinced myself I knew my subject completely—so who better to edit than myself? I read each chapter countless times until every word felt essential.

Then reality hit. Professional coaches who read my book sent back notes that gutted me. "Your introduction contradicts your third chapter." "I'm confused about your audience." "This concept needs more explanation." "Where's your evidence?"

I missed these issues because I wasn't reading what was actually written—I was reading what I thought I'd written. My mind automatically filled gaps that readers couldn't see. I couldn't spot contradictions because I understood nuances that never made it from my brain to the page.

What Professional Editing Actually Does

Professional editing doesn't change your voice—it amplifies it. It doesn't destroy your vision—it ensures others can see it.

Think of it like a musical performance. You might play perfectly in your living room, but a sound engineer knows how to make those notes reach the audience.

Professional editors provide:

Developmental Editing: They see your story's structure objectively. They know when your perfect chapter one belongs as chapter three. They feel where your pacing drags, where your themes tangle. In non-fiction, they understand when concepts need more scaffolding.

Line Editing: They catch rhythms you've gone deaf to from too many readings. They spot repetitions you can't see anymore. They feel where your language soars and where it stumbles.

Copy Editing: They find inconsistencies your brain automatically corrects—characters whose traits change, timelines that don't align. In non-fiction, they catch terminology shifts and examples that contradict your point.

Proofreading: They catch errors your eyes skip over—missing words your mind fills in, typos you'll never see because you know what you meant to write.

Why Professional Eyes Matter

Your book is a three-dimensional product, not just a collection of words. You've been staring at it so long, you've forgotten how to see it. You need someone who can:

- Question your assumptions
- Identify logical leaps
- Highlight repetitive language
- Expose structure weaknesses
- Test your arguments
- Notice pacing issues
- Flag inconsistencies
- See what you've grown blind to

When The Red Ink Feels Personal

Having an editor tell you that a whole chapter is off or paragraphs need to be removed feels like betrayal. We cling to our words like they're extensions of our identity. Instead of thinking, "This doesn't work—let's fix it," we get defensive, argue, or abandon the manuscript.

I've stood at that crossroads between ego and improvement. I've held feedback in trembling hands and had to decide: Will I protect my pride or serve my story?

Every word came from somewhere real. That scene your editor wants to cut? It's the last conversation with your father. That "unnecessary" character? She's built from pieces of your best friend. That lengthy description of a house? It's your grandmother's home, preserved in words because you couldn't save it in reality.

These aren't just words—they're fragments of your heart, moments you're trying to rescue from oblivion.

The Business of Better Books

Editing demands emotional intelligence, not just technical skill. You must separate yourself from your creation enough to see it objectively. Ask not "Is this beautiful?" but "Does this serve the reader?" Recognize that your most carefully crafted passages might be exactly what stands between your audience and your story's heart.

My first major edit letter was twelve pages of single-spaced suggestions. Two years of work questioned. My dream characters and polished scenes all called into question.

"This chapter doesn't serve the story." "This character dilutes the main conflict." "This subplot distracts from the core narrative." "This beautiful scene kills your pacing."

Each comment felt like an attack until I realized: My editor wasn't fighting against my story—she was fighting for it.

We hold onto words like memories—desperately, as if letting go means losing them forever. We argue for scenes that slow our story because we remember how long they took to write. We fight to keep characters that blur our focus because they've become real to us.

Professional editors see what we can't: the gap between our intention and execution, between what we meant to say and what we actually wrote, between our emotional connection to our story and the reader's experience.

When to Fight for Your Words (And When to Let Go)

When your editor suggests changes, ask yourself:

- Does this serve the story?
- Does it clarify meaning?
- Does it strengthen impact?
- Does it help readers?
- Does it maintain voice?
- Does it improve flow?

Fight for your words only when they:

- Are crucial to story meaning
- Maintain authentic voice
- Preserve cultural accuracy
- Support central themes
- Define key characters
- Drive essential plot points

Your story exists beneath the words you've layered over it. A good editor helps uncover it. They see beyond your attachment to what you've written and reveal what you're truly trying to express. They understand that often, our deepest insights get buried under the lesser ones we try to hold onto.

DO NOT SKIP PROFESSIONAL EDITING OR DISMISS FEEDBACK

From Feedback to Finished Product

Save those deleted scenes in another file if you must. Preserve them like pressed flowers—beautiful, brittle reminders of what once bloomed in your mind. But don't let them overshadow the living garden your story needs to become.

In the space between what you wrote and what your story needs to be, trust the hand that guides you toward the heart of it. Some words serve memory; others serve the story. Learning to distinguish between them elevates writing from personal expression to professional craft.

Confession: My first professionally edited book sat on my desktop for 5 years. The manuscript just languished there—a completed work that I couldn't bring myself to release. When Amazon launched Vella, I convinced myself I'd finally do something with it, uploading just five chapters with plans to continue. I never did. The project died there, half-birthed in a platform that couldn't save it from my hesitation.

This is what failure to launch looks like. Not the dramatic crash-and-burn, but the quiet neglect that kills more creative projects than rejection ever could. That manuscript represented thousands of dollars in editing, countless hours of writing, and a story I once believed in enough to invest in professionally. All wasted.

Do not do that. Those edits exist as stepping stones, not roadblocks. You poured your soul into that story - now it's time to wrestle with your emotions and make the necessary changes. When you've done the work, launch it. No holding back. No second-guessing. What readers crave is your authentic perspective, filtered through professional standards.

Your Words, Only Better

Your book deserves the time and resources necessary to achieve its full potential. Your readers deserve a polished, professional product. Your future self deserves the pride of knowing you launched with excellence, not regret.

Professional editing isn't an expense—it's an investment in your book's success and your reputation as an author. The feedback isn't an attack on your creativity—it's a bridge between your vision and your readers' experience.

Embrace the process. Wrestle with the suggestions. Make the hard choices. Your book will emerge stronger, clearer, and more powerful than you could have made it alone.

DO NOT RELY ONLY ON GRAMMAR TOOLS

The green lines snake through the manuscript like ivy—Grammar tools suggestions blooming in the margins. Each click promises perfection. Each automated fix whispers of efficiency.

But it's all a beautiful lie.

Beyond Algorithms

Between the lines of the story, in spaces where meaning breathes, lives something no algorithm can touch. No software can sense. No automated tool will ever understand.

Take this simple line: "Her heart broke when she saw him."

Most grammar tools give it a checkmark. Perfect grammar! No issues found!

But a human editor asks: Did her heart break like glass—sudden and sharp? Like bread—slow and crumbling? Like waves—rhythmic and eternal? Was it a clean break or a hairline fracture? Was this fresh pain or the final crack in something long splintered?

The software sees words. The editor sees worlds.

The Cost of Algorithmic Editing

Many manuscripts arrive "Grammar tool approved." Authors believe they only need a quick proofread before publishing. What editors often find is technically correct prose that never once risks greatness. Every sentence stands proper and plain, stripped of voice by algorithmic suggestions. Metaphors get flattened. Purposeful fragments connected with unnecessary conjunctions. The technical writing? Impeccable. The story? Lifeless.

What Grammar Tools Miss

Grammar checkers won't tell you:

- When a sentence is accurate but lifeless
- When dialogue sounds technically perfect but humanly impossible
- When description lacks sensory detail
- When pacing needs variation
- When emotional notes ring false
- When scenes lack tension despite grammatical completeness

These tools can't recognize:

- Your unique voice and stylistic choices
- The rhythm and music of your prose
- The power of calculated rule-breaking
- The difference between technically correct and emotionally true
- The complexity of tone and subtext

They mark everything that deviates from their programming. They would correct Faulkner's streams of consciousness, flatten Dickinson's distinctive punctuation, standardize Cummings' experimental forms.

The Damage of Blind Compliance

When writers run their work through grammar tracking tools without discernment, these programs can methodically destroy stylistic choices—suggesting removing line breaks, adding articles to staccato phrases, rewriting metaphors as simpler comparisons. Accepting all these changes causes a unique voice to disappear completely, sacrificed to algorithmic conformity.

Use Tools Wisely, Not Blindly

Yes, use these tools to catch:

- Spelling errors
- Basic punctuation mistakes
- Obvious grammatical issues
- Repeated words (when unintentional)
- Consistency problems

But recognize their limitations. They cannot:

- Evaluate voice
- Judge pacing
- Assess emotional impact
- Recognize deliberate style choices
- Understand context

The Role of Grammar Tools vs. Human Editors

Grammar tools are hammers, not sculptors. They help you construct, not craft. They identify errors, not meaning.

These digital assistants miss subtleties human editors catch immediately. They don't understand when a fragment creates necessary emphasis. They can't recognize when passive voice actually serves the narrative better than active. They flag repeated words without considering deliberate rhythmic or thematic choices.

Even their technical accuracy fails. Homonym errors slip past—their/there/they're might be grammatically correct while contextually wrong. Correctly spelled wrong words remain undetected. Subject-verb agreement in complex sentences confuses the algorithms.

The Solution: Balanced Editing

Good writing needs both technical accuracy and human insight. Both digital tools and living wisdom. Both automated checks and experienced understanding.

Use the software. But don't let it use you. Don't let its green lines become prison bars around your voice or its suggestions become chains around your creativity.

Words deserve more than algorithms. They deserve eyes that see, hearts that feel, and minds that understand the delicate balance between rules and art, correctness and meaning.

Professional editors bring both. Use your tools. Then find your editor.

DO NOT CUT CORNERS ON PRESENTATION: PROOFREADING AND FORMATTING MATTER

Your Book's Professional Polish: The Final Touches That Make or Break Your Success

I can still recall tearing into the package of my first indie book. I'd nailed the visual elements at last. The joy of spotting my name on that cover (physically printed) lasted exactly fourteen seconds—until I noticed a misspelled word in the dedication. A duplicated paragraph on one page. Worse yet, the Kindle edition was already available, and once the paperback became available one of the women from my writers' group decided the ideal way to alert me to the additional grammar mistakes was through an Amazon review.

I felt like my world was crushed.

A single typing error can make readers question your entire book. Every statement. Every assertion. Every commitment. If that glaring mistake slipped past you, what other errors might be hiding beneath? Only a handful of readers will overlook those blunders and continue on.

Meanwhile, brilliant manuscripts trapped in poor formatting are like gourmet food on a paper plate. Readers can spot the difference before turning a single page. Your words deserve better than default margins and whatever font came pre-installed. This isn't vanity—it's respect for your work and readers.

The Real Cost of Presentation Errors

A colleague of mine received this one-star review: "Great premise, important message, but so many typos I couldn't finish. If the author couldn't bother with basic proofreading, why should I bother reading?" The reviewer then listed twelve errors from the first fifty pages.

My colleague skipped professional proofreading to save $400. That decision ultimately cost her readers, credibility, and thousands in potential sales.

When readers buy your book, they expect the same quality as traditionally published titles. They don't care about your publishing journey—they care about value. Every formatting error shouts "amateur" to potential buyers. Your book's formatting is product packaging - sloppy exterior signals sloppy content.

Your Brain Works Against You

Here's the problem: Your brain knows what you meant to write, so it automatically corrects what you actually wrote. It fills in missing words, adjusts wrong tenses, and corrects misspelled names—all without telling you. This is why you can read your manuscript ten times and still miss errors that jump out to fresh eyes instantly.

The same applies to formatting. What looks perfect on your screen. The fonts are crisp, margins clean, cover striking. You're ready to publish.

Then you order a proof copy.

What arrives isn't what you expected. Text cut off, colors dull, spacing wrong, or paper quality disappointing. Your book might be too thin to print properly, leaving you scrambling to add pages.

Format-Specific Requirements You Can't Ignore

Ebook Formatting

Ebooks must adapt to everything from phones to e-readers. Watch for:

- Inconsistent paragraph formatting
- Missing or broken navigation
- Irregular spacing between sections
- Font embedding issues
- Image sizing problems
- Table formatting that breaks on small screens

Print Formatting

Physical books demand precision with:

- Proper margins (accounting for binding)
- Consistent spacing and indentation
- Header and footer placement
- Page numbering conventions
- Font selection appropriate to genre
- Image resolution (minimum 300dpi)
- Bleed settings for full-page images

Audiobook Formatting

Even audiobooks need formatting with:

- Chapter markers properly placed
- Consistent volume levels throughout
- Room tone matching between sessions
- Proper handling of footnotes, tables, and visual elements

The Professional Proofreading Process

After my humiliating first-book experience, I created a three-level verification system:

1. **Self-editing pass:** Reading aloud to catch obvious errors
2. **Software check:** Using tools like Grammarly, ProWritingAid, or Hemingway to flag potential issues
3. **Professional proofreader:** Hiring someone with fresh eyes and specialized training

The investment seemed steep at the time—but the resulting clean manuscript generated reviews that focused on my content rather than my errors.

Professional proofreaders look for:

Basic Elements:

- Spelling, grammar, and punctuation errors
- Consistency in hyphenation, capitalization, and number formatting
- Proper use of quotation marks and dialogue formatting
- Accurate citation formatting

Technical Verification:

- Headers, footers, and page numbers
- Table of contents accuracy
- Running heads consistency
- Figure and table numbering
- Footnote and endnote formatting

Professional Formatting Is Non-Negotiable

In self-publishing, content may be king, but formatting is the throne that elevates it. I've watched talented writers crash and burn because their books screamed "amateur hour" from twenty feet away. Not because their stories lacked substance—but because the packaging betrayed them. "I did it in Word" or

"I used a free app" aren't accomplishments; they're confessions.

The interior speaks before your words do. I once watched a woman pick up a self-published memoir with a stunning cover in a bookstore. She opened it, frowned slightly, flipped through a few pages, then returned it with a sigh before moving on. The cover did its job, but the interior—with shifting margins, inconsistent layouts, and random font changes—destroyed the promise of professionalism. She never even read the first paragraph.

The Financial Decision: DIY vs. Professional

You have two options: master formatting yourself or hire professionals.

DIY saves money upfront but costs more through:

- Learning curve time investment
- Software purchases
- Potential errors requiring reprints
- Lost sales from unprofessional appearance
- Damage to author reputation

Professional formatting typically costs $200-$800 depending on complexity—an investment that pays for itself through improved sales and saved time.

Professional formatters bring more than technical knowledge; they understand reader psychology, design principles, and industry standards. They know which fonts work for your genre, how to create balanced margins accounting for binding, and how to establish visual hierarchy that guides readers intuitively.

This Isn't Optional

Perfect proofreading isn't just about finding errors. It's about preserving reader trust. Protecting your credibility. Honoring your story.

Professional formatting isn't aesthetic preference—it's reader respect. Every technical choice either facilitates or frustrates that experience. Inconsistent fonts force readers' brains to constantly readjust. Poor line spacing makes tracking difficult. Misaligned headers create subtle visual discord that registers as unprofessional.

The market no longer forgives amateur presentation. Today's readers expect professional standards regardless of how you published. Your words merit the best possible presentation. When readers invest in your book, your presentation should enhance their experience, not distract from it.

The Pre-Publication Proofreading and Formatting Checklist

Before publishing:

1. Order a physical proof copy - never rely solely on digital previews
2. Read the entire book in print - errors are more visible on paper
3. Check all headers, footers, and page numbers

4. Verify chapter headings and table of contents
5. Confirm consistent margins and spacing
6. Test all hyperlinks in digital editions
7. View your ebook on multiple devices
8. Have someone else review the final version

This is your book. Your vision. Your legacy. It deserves to be presented with the same care you put into writing it. Your readers deserve an experience free from amateur distractions. Your message deserves a vessel that enhances rather than diminishes its power.

A book isn't just about words—it's about how those words reach the reader. Even beautiful prose can't overcome the barriers of a messy, unprofessional layout or distracting errors. Format professionally, proofread meticulously, or watch your publishing dreams fade—your choice, but the consequences are non-negotiable.

DO NOT REWRITE INDEFINITELY

The endless pursuit of perfection claims countless manuscripts every year. Authors trapped in revision cycles watch their work grow stagnant as they polish the same sentences, restructure the same scenes, and refine the same character arcs ad infinitum. Version after version accumulates in digital folders, each slightly different but never deemed "ready" for publication. What begins as necessary improvement evolves into a counterproductive pattern that prevents books from ever reaching their intended audience.

This isn't revision anymore. This is hiding.

Every writer knows this destructive dance. Change a word, change it back. Move scenes around like furniture. Add description, strip it away, add different description. Polish sentences until they shine like glass and become just as fragile.

With each obsessive pass, the manuscript weakens like fabric washed too many times. The voice fades. The passion bleeds out word by word.

Many authors spend years on a single book—not from necessity, but from inability to declare it complete. One exceptional novelist rewrote her ending seventeen times, each version more technically perfect and less emotionally impactful than the last. When she finally published (only after having a non-negotiable deadline imposed), readers connected most powerfully with scenes she'd barely touched since her first draft.

The Warning Signs You're Hiding, Not Revising

- You've rewritten the same chapter more than three times
- You change things, then change them back to how they were
- You've lost perspective on whether changes improve the work
- You can quote entire passages from memory
- Beta readers' feedback no longer surprises you
- You're making only microscopic changes
- You've stopped sending the manuscript to readers
- You dread the thought of anyone seeing it
- You can't articulate what still needs fixing—just that it's "not ready"
- Your revision process no longer has clear goals

The Real Barriers Keeping You Stuck

Endless revision isn't dedication to craft—it's avoidance of vulnerability. As long as your book remains "in progress," it can't be judged, can't fail, can't succeed in ways that might change your life. It exists safely in potential, never risking actual existence in the world where others might interpret it in ways you can't control.

Professional authors establish clear revision boundaries: a specific number of developmental passes, line edits, and final reviews. They set firm deadlines and enlist accountability partners. When doubt inevitably creeps in—when they want "just one more" major revision—they ask themselves: "Am I improving the book or hiding from publishing it?" The answer is often uncomfortable but clarifying.

Know When to Stop

Your book is ready when:

- The story fundamentally works
- Characters act consistently with their established traits
- The pacing serves the genre and story needs
- The beginning hooks and the ending satisfies
- Line-level prose is clear and effective
- Beta readers focus on preferences rather than problems
- You're making changes that neither you nor readers can detect

- Professional editing has addressed structural and mechanical issues
- You've implemented feedback from target readers

Final Steps Before Release

1. Set a non-negotiable publication date
2. Schedule your final proofreading pass
3. Write your book description and marketing materials
4. Plan your launch strategy
5. Remove your ability to make further changes (send to formatter/publisher)

Your book will never achieve perfection. It will either be finished or forgotten. Every successful author knows: Books aren't finished—they're surrendered. At some point, you must let your story live in the world instead of dying in endless revision.

The most powerful books aren't technically flawless—they're authentically human, full of voice and depth. They prioritize connection over perfection, impact over immaculateness.

Set your deadline. Mark your date. Plan your launch. Stop rewriting and start releasing.

Your readers aren't waiting for the perfect book. They're waiting for YOUR book—the one only you can write, with all its unique perspective and particular beauty. They're waiting for the story that will speak to them in ways no other story can. They'll never find it while it's trapped in revision limbo on your computer.

Your readers are waiting. Stop making them.

DO NOT PUBLISH WITH INCONSISTENCIES

Your protagonist switches eye colors mid-book. Your villain relocates their lair between chapters. Your hero suddenly gains a sister after being an only child. A one-time magical amulet works three times. A critical clue appears after the case is solved.

And just like that, your reader is gone forever.

When a character's mother dies in chapter two, then casually eats dinner with the family in chapter seventeen, readers notice. Their response isn't just confusion—it's a fundamental breach of trust. The unspoken message is clear: "If you missed something this significant, I no longer trust what else might be broken in your world."

This isn't about typos or grammar. It's about trust fractures.

Common Story-Breaking Inconsistencies

Brilliant stories die from these wounds:

- Character details that change (eye color, scars, backgrounds)
- Timeline impossibilities (events happening out of sequence)
- Worldbuilding contradictions (rules that shift without explanation)
- Plot holes (unresolved questions, vanishing storylines)
- Unexplained character knowledge (information they couldn't have)
- Setting relocations (rooms changing layout, distances altering)
- Ability inconsistencies (skills appearing and disappearing)

One principle remains constant: "Readers will follow you anywhere if they trust you know where you're going." Without that trust, even the most beautiful prose can't save you.

What Readers Track (Even When You Don't)

Your readers are tracking everything:

- Physical character descriptions
- Relationship histories
- Emotional states and development
- Time passage and sequences

- Geographic locations and distances
- Rules of your world (magic, technology, social systems)
- Item possession and placement

They notice when weather changes randomly, injuries heal too quickly, characters know information they couldn't possibly have, or objects appear without explanation.

Professional Tracking Systems

Professional story tracking requires:

Character bibles with:

- Physical descriptions (height, weight, eye/hair color, distinguishing marks)
- Background details (education, family, significant events)
- Personality traits and quirks
- Skills and abilities
- Relationships to other characters
- Character arcs and growth markers

Detailed timelines marking:

- Chapter-by-chapter events
- Time of day for scenes
- Days/weeks/months of story progress
- Character ages and birthdays
- Historical events affecting the story

- Season and weather conditions

World mapping:

- Physical locations and distances
- Building layouts and room descriptions
- Travel times between locations
- Environmental features
- Cultural boundaries and regions

Rule documentation:

- Magic system limitations and costs
- Technology capabilities and restrictions
- Social customs and taboos
- Political structures
- Economic systems

Digital Tools for Consistency Management

Professional authors increasingly rely on specialized software:

- Aeon Timeline for complex chronologies
- World Anvil for worldbuilding documentation
- Scrivener's metadata tracking
- Campfire Pro for character and world management
- Custom spreadsheets and databases

The Beta Reader Consistency Check

Before publishing, implement a systematic consistency review:

- Assign specific readers to track particular elements
- Create questionnaires targeting potential inconsistencies
- Hold character-focused feedback sessions
- Compare timeline reconstructions from different readers
- Ask readers to map the story world from memory

Professional Editorial Scrutiny

Professional editors check for:

- Timeline integrity across the full manuscript
- Character consistency throughout all scenes
- Setting details that remain stable
- Plot logic that holds under scrutiny
- Worldbuilding rules applied consistently
- Foreshadowing that connects to payoffs

The High Cost of Inconsistency

Each inconsistency forces readers to stop and question, push past confusion, make mental adjustments, or create their own explanations. Every time they do, they step out of your story. Too many breaks, and they're gone for good.

An author who dismissed concerns about seventeen timeline inconsistencies in her thriller learned this lesson through reviews flooded with complaints. Readers had noticed. They had cared. And many decided her next book wasn't worth the frustration.

The Credibility Bank Account

Think of reader trust as a bank account. Small inconsistencies make withdrawals. Too many withdrawals, and you're overdrawn—readers abandon the book and possibly your entire catalog.

Professional consistency requires:

- Meticulous tracking from the first draft
- Regular review of story elements
- Dedicated consistency editing passes
- Beta readers focused on continuity
- Professional editing support

Don't trust your memory. Don't assume you'll catch errors. Create systems. Use tools. Build checks.

This isn't about perfectionism—it's about maintaining the dream, protecting the illusion, preserving the sacred trust between writer and reader.

Make your story bulletproof. Check every detail. Verify every claim. Confirm every connection.

Your readers are paying attention. You must do the same.

IV. COVER DESIGN & BOOK FORMATTING MISTAKES

DO NOT NEGLECT SPINE AND BACK COVER

Your book is a three-dimensional product, not just a pretty front cover. When you neglect the spine and back cover, you've created an incomplete product that signals "amateur" to industry professionals and readers alike.

Consider this breakdown: Your front cover is the introduction, your spine is the handshake, and your back cover is the closing argument that convinces someone to buy. Every element must be intentional and polished.

Many authors invest thousands into stunning front covers only to throw together mediocre spines and back covers as an afterthought. Then they wonder why bookstores won't stock their books or why browsers don't become buyers.

The simple fact is: You might have written an exceptional novel, but if your spine disappears on a bookshelf or your back cover fails to deliver a compelling reason to read, your masterpiece will remain undiscovered.

The Spine: Your Ambassador on Crowded Shelves

Walk through any bookstore. What do you see first? Spines. Rows upon rows of books competing for attention. Only the ones that stand out get pulled from the shelf.

Your spine needs to be:

- Legible from a distance
- Color-contrasted for visibility
- Properly aligned without bleeding into the front or back
- Correctly sized for your book's thickness
- Consistent with your overall brand

The text direction matters too—typically top to bottom in the U.S. and bottom to top in the U.K. Your font should match or complement your cover typography for visual cohesion.

For thin books (under 100 pages), you face additional challenges. If your book doesn't have enough pages for spine text, compensate with stronger front and back covers. Don't force text where it doesn't belong—work with what you have.

Spine Design Psychology

Research shows readers spend only 3-5 seconds scanning shelves before focusing on specific spines. The most effective spines:

- Use high contrast colors that stand out
- Include a distinctive design element or pattern
- Feature an author logo or publisher emblem
- Maintain readability even at a distance
- Show genre awareness through design elements

The Back Cover: Closing the Sale

Once a reader picks up your book, the back cover must convert curiosity into commitment. It needs to answer one crucial question: "Why should I spend my time and money on this?"

A professional back cover includes:

- Compelling book description (blurb)
- Author bio and photo
- Relevant endorsements or reviews
- Genre identifiers
- ISBN and barcode
- Publisher information

The layout is critical too. Balance elements with adequate white space. Make text readable but not oversized. Maintain consistent design elements from your front cover.

Back Cover Copy That Sells

The most effective back cover copy follows a proven structure:

- Hook sentence that grabs attention (1-2 lines)

- Compelling situation or character introduction (2-3 sentences)
- Core conflict that drives the story (1-2 sentences)
- Stakes that make readers care (1-2 sentences)
- Promise of the reading experience without revealing the ending

Keep the total word count under 200 words. Use short paragraphs with breathing room between them. Choose an easily readable font no smaller than 10pt.

Technical Requirements You Can't Ignore

Different platforms have different specifications:

- IngramSpark, KDP, and local printers all require specific measurements
- Account for bleed areas (typically 0.125" beyond trim size)
- Ensure proper spine width calculation based on page count and paper weight
- Allow for barcode placement in the correct position
- Maintain safe zones for critical text (at least 0.25" from edges)

When creating your full cover:

- Use CMYK color mode for print (not RGB)
- Maintain at least 300 DPI resolution
- Account for barcode placement (typically bottom right)

- Ensure proper PDF export settings for print

If this overwhelms you, hire a professional designer. Yes, it costs money, but consider it an investment in your book's success. A well-designed package opens doors to bookstores, libraries, and readers who might otherwise pass you by.

Look, if you're set on handling the design yourself, start with the pro templates from your chosen publishing platform. They'll lay out exactly where everything needs to go, from the measurement specs to those critical bleed zones. Been there, done that, and these templates are lifesavers when you're navigating margins and text placement.

Coordinating Front, Spine, and Back

The three components should work together as a unified design:

- Use consistent typography across all elements
- Maintain color palette harmony
- Extend design elements across all three surfaces
- Ensure visual flow that guides the eye
- Create a cohesive package that feels intentional

What Makes a Professional Package

Readers browse bookshelves, pulling volumes based solely on spine design, then making purchase decisions after thirty seconds with the back cover. Bookstore owners regularly reject otherwise good self-published books because of spine miscalculations or amateurish back covers.

Your book deserves better than to be dismissed over technical oversights. Your story deserves the chance to be discovered. Your hard work deserves the respect of a complete, professional package.

You didn't write half a book, so don't design half a cover. In a world of endless reading choices, your book's complete package might be the difference between being passed over and being purchased. Make every element count.

DO NOT CHOOSE ILLEGIBLE FONTS

Fonts whisper before words even speak. They shape how we absorb a message, how our eyes move across the page, how our minds settle into a story's rhythm. They guide us—or push us away.

A book with too many fonts can look like a ransom note. Five different fonts—one for chapter headings, another for subheadings, body text, block quotes, and a decorative script for each chapter's first letter—might seem sophisticated but creates a design disaster. Readers frequently mention "distracting typography" more than actual content. One reader noted, "I couldn't focus on the story because the fonts kept shouting at me."

Too many self-published authors treat fonts as decorative afterthoughts rather than fundamental design elements. They pick ornate fonts because they look fancy, playful ones because they feel fun, bold ones because they want to stand out.

But standing out isn't the goal. Readability is.

The fastest way to look like an amateur is to make your reader work harder than necessary.

Nobody will struggle through a book just because you liked how a font looked in your draft. Period.

The Cost of Poor Font Choices

Illegible fonts break reading flow. Script fonts might be beautiful on wedding invitations but become exhausting across an entire book. Thick, blocky letters work for billboards, not 300 pages of text. Unusual typefaces might seem creative, but creativity should never sacrifice clarity.

When readers have to squint, slow down, or rest their eyes after a few paragraphs—they'll put your book down.

The wrong font doesn't just make your book look unprofessional. It makes it unreadable.

A historical novelist once used a decorative Gothic font throughout her novel because it "felt authentic to the medieval time period." Visually, it resembled an illuminated manuscript. Practically, it was unreadable beyond a page. When standard serif fonts with Gothic reserved for headings were suggested, she protested: "But it won't look medieval anymore!" True—but it would actually get read, which seemed more important.

The One Rule That Matters: Simplicity

Too many fonts create visual chaos. A book isn't a flyer or social media post—it's a structured reading experience.

Stick to two or three fonts maximum:

- One for body text
- One for headings (chapter titles, section breaks)
- Optionally, one for special elements (quotes, footnotes)

Anything beyond this creates distraction. Your book should flow, not feel like a design experiment.

Font Selection Fundamentals

Body text must be easy on the eyes. That means clean, classic fonts with even spacing.

For print books, these serif fonts have stood the test of time:

- Garamond
- Baskerville
- Caslon
- Palatino
- Minion Pro

For ebooks, consider:

- Georgia
- Literata

- Bookerly
- Caecilia
- Source Serif Pro

Size matters too. Print books typically use 11-12 point text. Ebooks should have reflowable text. Avoid extremes—too small strains eyes, too large wastes space and looks amateur.

Advanced Typography Considerations

- Line spacing (leading): 120-150% of your font size
- Margins: Minimum 0.75" for print books, wider on binding edge
- Text alignment: Justified for print, left-aligned for digital
- Paragraph spacing: Consistent throughout
- Hyphenation: Use sparingly to avoid awkward gaps
- Widows and orphans: Eliminate single words at page beginnings/ends

Match Your Genre's Typography Language

Readers expect certain typography styles based on what they're reading:

- Thrillers often use sans-serif headings with serif body text
- Literary fiction tends toward classic, elegant serifs throughout
- Romance may use slightly more decorative chapter headings

- Science fiction frequently employs clean, modern sans-serif
- Children's books use larger, more approachable fonts

Nonfiction follows similar patterns. Self-help books need clean, energetic fonts. Business books require professional typography. Memoirs often use classic typefaces that don't distract from personal narratives.

Accessibility Considerations

- Avoid fonts smaller than 11pt
- Maintain strong contrast between text and background
- Choose fonts with distinct letter shapes (avoid ones where "I" and "l" look identical)
- Consider dyslexia-friendly fonts for educational materials
- Ensure adequate line spacing for readability

Common Mistakes to Avoid

- Decorative fonts for body text
- Mixing too many different typefaces
- Using all caps for long passages
- Inconsistent spacing between chapters or sections
- Centering body text
- Random font size changes
- Colored text that reduces contrast

The best fonts go unnoticed. They don't call attention to themselves. They simply guide the reader through the experience.

A thriller should feel tense before the first word. A self-help book should feel inspiring from the presentation alone. A romance novel should exude warmth before the story begins.

That won't happen if your book looks cluttered, unreadable, or chaotic.

Choose wisely. Simplify. Let your words shine, not your fonts.

DO NOT DESIGN YOUR OWN COVER OR USE AMATEUR IMAGES

Your Book's First Impression: Why Professional Visuals Determine Success

That photo editing software looks tempting. Those design templates seem easy. "I wrote the entire book—surely I can handle one simple cover design."

Stop right there.

Many authors make this mistake with their first book. They perfect the manuscript for months, then design a cover in Canva over a weekend. It might look decent to an untrained eye. Friends call it "creative" and "unique." But the market response tells the real story.

Your book sits on a shelf surrounded by countless others. A potential reader picks it up and flips through the first few pages. You have thirty seconds—probably less—to make them care. What they see in those moments determines whether your book goes home with them or returns to the shelf, unread.

Why Amateur Covers Kill Book Sales

Professional designers don't sugarcoat it: "Your cover signals self-help, not memoir. The colors evoke corporate training, not emotional journey. At thumbnail size, your title is completely unreadable." A professionally designed cover that accurately signals genre and emotional tone can dramatically increase sales.

Homemade covers compete with professionally designed books on Amazon. Professional covers are crafted by artists who've mastered typography, color theory, composition, and market psychology. That free template? Thousands of other authors are using it right now, creating a sea of identical, amateur-looking books.

The Hidden Cost of Poor Images

Low-resolution images are silent credibility killers. Readers can't articulate why pictures look wrong, but they feel it. Those jagged edges and washed-out colors trigger an unconscious decision: this book isn't worth my time. They associate visual sloppiness with content sloppiness—and move on.

When a poetry collection arrives from the printer, photographs that looked perfect on a computer screen can appear pixelated, murky, and amateur on paper. Bookstores might refuse to stock a book not because the content isn't good, but because the images scream "homemade."

DO NOT DESIGN YOUR OWN COVER OR USE AMATEUR IMAGES

Five Non-Negotiable Rules for Book Visuals

1. Study Your Competition Relentlessly

Open the bestsellers in your genre. What quality of images do they include? How are they positioned? What style predominates? You're not copying—you're meeting the minimum standard your readers expect.

2. Test Before You Commit

Don't settle for the first option. If hiring a photographer or illustrator, demand samples. Ensure they understand your vision and audience. The cheapest option costs more when it tanks your book's credibility.

3. Google Is Not Your Personal Image Bank

You CANNOT just Google images and place them in your book. Every image online is either:

- Copyrighted (requiring permission and often payment)
- Licensed (with specific terms you must follow)
- Public domain (free but must be verified)
- Creative Commons (with varying usage restrictions)

Use legal stock sites like Shutterstock, Adobe Stock, Depositphotos, or Unsplash—and still check their licensing terms. Better yet, invest in original artwork.

4. Resolution Requirements Are Non-Negotiable

Images must be at least 300 dots per inch (DPI) for print. Anything less will look professional on screen and pathetic in print. Test by zooming in—does it stay sharp? Print a sample—are the edges clean? If not, start over.

For ebooks, images need lower resolution (72-150 DPI) but must maintain proper proportions and clarity. Different devices display differently, so test on multiple screens before finalizing.

5. Never, Ever Stretch Images

When you drag image corners to make them fit, you're announcing to readers: "I don't know what I'm doing." Images distort. Proportions warp. Credibility vanishes.

Instead:

- Crop properly, maintaining aspect ratio
- Resize using professional tools that maintain quality
- Replace images that don't fit rather than forcing them

What Professional Designers Know That You Don't

Professional cover designers understand:

- **Genre expectations:** Every genre has visual language that signals content to readers. Romance covers use different color palettes and typography than thrillers.
- **Market positioning:** Cover design places your book

alongside comparable titles, telling readers, "If you liked that book, you'll like mine."

• **Psychological triggers:** Certain colors, compositions, and font choices trigger specific emotional responses.

• **Technical requirements:** Bleed areas, spine width calculations, and trim specifications require technical expertise.

• **Thumbnail optimization:** Most readers first see your cover as a tiny image on a screen, requiring specific design approaches.

Your Cover's Multiple Functions

Your cover must achieve multiple goals simultaneously:

- Instantly communicate genre and tone
- Work at multiple sizes from thumbnail to physical book
- Appeal to your specific target audience
- Support your brand identity
- Stand out while fitting genre expectations
- Remain readable and compelling on screens and in print

Budget-Friendly Solutions

If budget is tight, consider:

- Pre-made covers from professional designers (often $50-300)

- Design contests on sites like 99designs
- Student designers from art schools
- Bartering with professional designers (offering editing, promotion, etc.)
- Simplified designs that require less custom artwork

The Amazon Test

Take a moment to conduct your own experiment. Visit Amazon and search for books in your genre. Look at the bestsellers, then search for less popular titles in the same category. Notice how the professional covers instantly communicate genre, tone, and quality. They pull your eye and make you want to click.

Your book deserves to stand out—but for the right reasons, with professional execution that signals quality before the reader reads a single word.

You poured everything into your words—your time, energy, late nights and early mornings. You've crafted sentences until they sang and shaped characters until they breathed.

Don't undermine it all with amateur visuals.

You're not here to blend in with thousands of amateur authors making the same rookie mistakes. You're here to be taken seriously. To make a statement with every element of your book.

Your visuals are promises. Make them promises you can keep.

DO NOT VIOLATE FONT LICENSES

Font Licensing Can Make or Break Your Publishing Career

Fonts are everywhere—on book covers, in interior layouts, on promotional graphics. With so many free font websites and design tools like Canva and Photoshop offering an endless selection, it's easy to assume that if you can download a font, you can use it. But that assumption could cost you.

Many authors have faced serious consequences after using fonts without proper licensing. One historical book featuring a stunning cursive typeface for chapter titles was pulled from distribution six months after becoming an Amazon bestseller when the typeface creator threatened legal action. The font had been labeled "free" but was only free for personal use—not commercial applications.

Don't be fooled—just because you can access a font doesn't mean it's yours to use commercially. Numerous typefaces require proper licensing for publication, and using one without proper permissions can result in copyright infringement, legal headaches, and potentially having your book yanked from retail platforms.

The publishing world is littered with similar stories—authors who unwittingly used unlicensed fonts and paid the price. One romance writer had to recall and destroy three hundred print copies after discovering the script font on her cover required a commercial license she didn't possess. Another author found his ebook pulled from multiple platforms because he'd embedded a font that was only licensed for print use, not digital.

Why Font Licensing Matters

Not All Fonts Are Free. Many fonts you find online are only free for personal use—which means you can use them for projects like personal documents, invitations, or school assignments, but NOT for anything you intend to sell (like a book). That beautiful script you used for your chapter headings might be fine for a family newsletter but using it in a commercial book is a different matter entirely.

Using Unlicensed Fonts Can Lead to Legal Issues. If a font designer or foundry discovers that you've used their font commercially without a license, they can:

- Issue cease and desist orders
- Demand licensing fees (often with penalties)

- Pursue legal action for copyright infringement
- Require you to recall and reprint materials

Font designers, like all creatives, deserve compensation for their work.

Amazon, IngramSpark, and Other Platforms Have Rules. Self-publishing platforms require authors to own the rights to all elements of their book, including fonts. If you use an unlicensed font on your cover or interior, your book could be removed from distribution. Many authors lose months of marketing momentum when their books suddenly disappear from retailers due to font licensing issues.

Understanding Font Copyright Protection

Unlike other creative works, fonts exist in a unique legal space:

- The letter shapes (design) may not be copyrightable in some jurisdictions
- The font software (digital files) is almost always protected by copyright
- The font name is typically trademarked
- Usage rights vary between personal and commercial applications
- Different countries have different legal protections for typefaces

This complexity creates confusion for many authors. The key point: while the letter shapes themselves might not be copyrighted in some countries, the font software (the file you download) almost always is.

How to Check Font Licenses

Before using a font in your book, make sure you understand its license:

Look at the Font's Download Page. Fonts from sites like Google Fonts are usually free for commercial use. Fonts from sites like DaFont or 1001 Fonts often have restrictions—many are only free for personal use unless you buy a license. Always check the font's license description before downloading. Don't just look for the word "free"—look specifically for "free for commercial use."

Check Font Licenses in Design Software. When in doubt, check the terms of service or contact customer support.

Purchase Commercial Licenses from Font Foundries. If a font is not free for commercial use, buy a license from a legitimate font website like MyFonts, Fontspring, or Creative Market. Yes, this adds to your production costs, but it's far less expensive than legal issues later.

What to Do If You Already Used an Unlicensed Font

If you've already published your book and later realize the font isn't licensed for commercial use, act fast to avoid legal issues:

- Replace the unlicensed font immediately in future editions

- Contact the font creator to purchase retroactive licensing if available
- Consult with a publishing attorney if you've received legal notices
- Be prepared to redesign your cover or interior as needed

Best Paid Fonts for Professional Books

When investing in professional typography for your book, consider these industry standards:

- Minion Pro: Versatile serif perfect for fiction and nonfiction
- Garamond Premier Pro: Classic with multiple weights for flexibility
- Baskerville: Distinguished serif with excellent readability
- Adobe Caslon Pro: Traditional serif with a timeless feel
- Palatino: Elegant with excellent readability across formats

Font Licensing for International Distribution

If your book will be distributed internationally, be aware that:

- Copyright laws vary significantly between countries
- Some nations offer stronger typeface protections than others

- Multi-platform licenses may require different permissions
- Embedding rights must be specified for e-book distribution
- Font usage in marketing materials often requires separate licensing

Protect Your Book, Protect Your Brand

Your book is your business. And just like any business, cutting corners can lead to consequences. Don't assume all fonts are free. Check the licenses, invest in the right fonts, and ensure your book is legally compliant. Because the last thing you want is to have your book taken down—not because of your words, but because of your font choice.

DO NOT SEND MIXED VISUAL MESSAGES: COVER DESIGN THAT SELLS

Less Is More: Your Book Cover Isn't a Cereal Box

Book titles sometimes aren't just long—they're entire paragraphs masquerading as titles. Authors often defend lengthy titles with the same explanation: "I need to explain what's inside."

The reality is simple: your book cover has about three seconds to make an impression. Three. That's it. It's a glance, not a conversation. Readers don't have time to decode your miniature essay before deciding if they're interested.

Many marketing book covers fail because they cram everything on there—title, subtitle, tagline, reviews, credentials, and even bullet points listing what readers would learn. When sales flatline and publishing consultants evaluate such covers, their feedback is direct: "Your cover looks like a classified ad. Readers can't process all that in the split second they're deciding whether to click."

Your cover's job isn't to explain—it's to entice. Books with just the title, author name, and one powerful image start selling because people can instantly grasp the concept without being overwhelmed with text they have no time to read.

The Color Code: Why Genre-Appropriate Colors Matter

Colors tell your book's story before readers read a single word. They aren't decorative—they're functional. The color scheme sends immediate signals about genre, tone, and content that either attract your target audience or push them away.

Many authors learn this lesson the hard way. A business leadership book with playful, bright orange and lime green colors might reflect the author's energetic personality, but when professionals scroll past it because it looks like a children's book, the disconnect becomes clear. The thoughtful, innovative content never reaches its intended audience of executives and business leaders.

This is a common amateur mistake. Choosing colors because you like them, not because they serve your book's market position. A personal love for neon green means nothing if you're writing historical romance. The black-and-red scheme you find dramatic will actively repel readers looking for a children's book.

Your cover isn't about your preferences. It's about meeting reader expectations.

Why Text Overload Kills Sales

Too much text destroys your book's chances for three specific reasons:

> **1. Visual overwhelm:** Readers can't process multiple elements in the few seconds they look at your cover. Each added line reduces the impact of essential information.
> **2. Thumbnail illegibility:** Most buyers first see your book as a tiny image on a screen. Dense text becomes unreadable, turning your carefully crafted cover into a blurry mess.
> **3. Professionalism signals:** Cluttered covers signal amateur production to industry professionals. Bookstores, reviewers, and media outlets make snap judgments about your book's quality based on these visual cues.

The Emotional Language of Color

Colors trigger specific emotional responses:

- **Blues:** Trust, calm, stability, professionalism
- **Reds:** Passion, urgency, danger, excitement
- **Greens:** Growth, wealth, nature, renewal
- **Yellows:** Optimism, warmth, energy, attention
- **Purples:** Luxury, spirituality, imagination, royalty
- **Blacks:** Sophistication, mystery, power, elegance
- **Whites:** Purity, simplicity, cleanliness, minimalism

Choose the wrong color and you send the wrong emotional signal. An inspirational book with ominous colors creates cognitive dissonance. Readers feel the disconnect even if they can't articulate why.

When authors design a tender coming-of-age novel with harsh oranges and blacks to "stand out," it certainly does—to all the wrong people. Horror fans click, feel misled by the description, and leave. Meanwhile, literary fiction readers who would have loved the story never even notice it. Switching to soft blues and gentle contrasts helps the actual audience finally find the book.

Genre-Specific Color Expectations

Study bestsellers in your genre and you'll notice consistent color patterns:

Thriller/Mystery: Dark backgrounds (black, navy, deep red) with high-contrast text. Creates tension and intrigue.

Romance:

• Contemporary: Soft pinks, teals, purples with modern typography

• Historical: Rich jewel tones, golds, and period-appropriate visuals

• Erotic: Deep purples, blacks, and reds with sensual imagery

Science Fiction:

• Hard sci-fi: Blues, blacks, metallic silvers with technical elements

- Space opera: Deep space blacks, nebula purples, starfield backgrounds
- Near future: Teals, whites, minimalist designs with single symbolic elements

Fantasy:

- Epic: Rich golds, deep blues, symbolic imagery
- Urban: City nightscapes, neon accents, street-level perspectives
- YA: Vibrant colors with symbolic central images

Nonfiction:

- Business: Blues, blacks, and neutrals with clean typography
- Self-help: Inspirational colors (yellows, light blues) with aspirational imagery
- Memoir: Softer, reflective palettes with personal imagery

What Your Cover Actually Needs

Strip your cover down to these essentials:

- Clear, legible title (visible at thumbnail size)
- Your author name
- A single compelling visual element
- Genre-appropriate color scheme

Everything else is probably excessive. Test your cover at thumbnail size. If any text blurs together, simplify further.

The Perfect Cover Balance

Let your design elements work for you. If your book is a thriller, the mood should be apparent without needing "A Heart-Pounding Thriller!" spelled out. Your imagery should communicate as much as your words.

The best covers use:

- **Negative space** to highlight key elements
- **Font hierarchies** that guide the eye
- **Symbolic imagery** that conveys theme
- **Color psychology** appropriate to genre
- **Composition** that creates visual interest

What to Remove Right Now

Take a hard look at your cover. If it has any of these, consider cutting:

- Lengthy subtitles
- Author credentials
- Multiple images or complex scenes
- Taglines or slogans
- Review quotes
- Awards or badges (unless major)
- Background textures that compete with text

Your cover is a billboard, not a brochure. If readers have to work to understand it, they'll keep scrolling.

Professional covers feature minimal text with genre-appropriate colors that enhance rather than distract. They use strong title placement, intentional spacing, and cohesive design where words and imagery work together.

Remember: You're not competing for a reader's time. You're competing for their attention. A clean cover with the right colors tells readers instantly what experience awaits inside your book.

Your book deserves the right visual language. Speak directly to your intended audience with appropriate colors and clean, focused design. They'll hear you loud and clear—and reach for your book.

DO NOT SKIP PROFESSIONAL PROOF COPIES

When Print Reality Crushes Digital Expectations

Your masterpiece looks flawless on screen—crisp fonts, clean margins, striking cover. You hover over that publish button, convinced your work is print-ready.

Then the proof copy arrives.

The text is cut off. Colors look muddy. Spacing is weird. The paper feels cheap. Your "book" is so thin it barely qualifies as a pamphlet. Your stomach sinks.

Ordering a professional proof copy isn't optional—it's mandatory. Printing at home is not a substitute.

Home Printing vs. Professional Proofs

New authors often try to save money by printing test copies at home. This creates a dangerous illusion of readiness. Your home printer cannot:

- Reproduce professional binding effects
- Accurately show bleed areas and trim lines
- Display true CMYK colors as they'll appear in print
- Replicate the actual paper stock your book will use
- Show spine alignment issues
- Demonstrate how images will actually render

What looks acceptable on your home-printed version may be completely unacceptable in the actual printed book.

The Digital-to-Print Reality Check

Your screen displays RGB colors—bright, vibrant, backlit. Print uses CMYK—always slightly different, often darker and less saturated. Those deep blues, reds, and purples you love? They might look completely different in print.

Text that's readable on your 27-inch monitor might require a magnifying glass in a paperback. Your older readers will hate you for this. Most printed books use 11-12pt fonts for body text—check yours before finalizing.

Print Production Realities Most Authors Miss

Technical Nightmares Waiting to Happen:

- Interior margins too narrow for binding
- Images too close to edges getting cut off
- Font embedding issues causing substitution
- Spine width calculations being incorrect
- Resolution problems making images pixelated
- Transparency effects rendering incorrectly

Margins, spacing, and bleed aren't suggestions—they're engineering requirements. Use the templates provided by KDP or IngramSpark. They account for binding physics that your design software doesn't understand.

Got a thin manuscript? You might not have enough pages to physically print a book:

- KDP requires a minimum of 24 pages
- IngramSpark requires at least 18 pages
- For spine printing, you typically need 100+ pages
- Perfect binding works best with 80+ pages

Many authors have to scramble at the last minute, adding front matter, back matter, or adjusting formatting just to meet these minimums. It's stressful and often leads to rushed decisions that damage your book's quality.

The Cost-Benefit Reality

Yes, professional proofs cost money:

- $5-15 for a proof copy
- Shipping fees
- Potential revision and reproof costs
- Time delays in your publishing schedule

But consider the alternative costs:

- Negative reviews mentioning poor production quality
- Lost readers who won't try your next book

- Embarrassment when showing your book to others
- Potential reprint costs to fix major errors
- Damage to your professional reputation

One professional proof pays for itself by preventing just one negative review or lost sale.

The Professional Proof Review Process

When that proof arrives, check:

- Cover colors, clarity, and positioning
- Spine alignment and readability
- Interior margins (especially the gutter)
- Font size and readability throughout
- Image quality and positioning
- Page numbering accuracy
- Running headers/footers alignment
- Overall binding quality and durability
- Paper quality and opacity
- Trim alignment on all edges

First impression test:

- Hand your book to someone unfamiliar with it
- Watch their reaction as they examine it
- Ask what they notice first (positive or negative)
- Note any confusion or hesitation they show

Cover evaluation:

- Check colors in different lighting conditions
- Ensure text is readable from 3 feet away
- Verify barcode scans properly
- Confirm spine text is centered
- Look for any printing defects or alignment issues

Interior inspection:

- Read several random pages completely
- Check for consistent spacing throughout
- Verify headers and page numbers align
- Test readability in normal reading light
- Confirm no text is cut off at margins

Binding quality check:

- Open the book fully and check the binding
- Verify pages don't fall out when flexed
- Check for even glue distribution
- Test if the book lies flat when open
- Ensure the cover doesn't separate from spine

Production comparison:

- Place your book next to similar professionally published titles
- Compare paper quality, cover finish, and binding
- Note any obvious quality differences
- Check how your book feels compared to others

The Physical Experience Matters

Books aren't just files—they're physical objects meant to be held, flipped through, stuffed in bags, and displayed on shelves. If your book doesn't feel right in hand, readers will notice. If it looks amateur, it will sell like an amateur product.

Plan Ahead for Proof Review

Allow sufficient time in your publication schedule:

- Order proof at least 3-4 weeks before planned launch
- Build in time for corrections and a second proof if needed
- Account for shipping delays, especially during busy seasons
- Reserve 1-2 days for thorough evaluation
- Add time for professional feedback if possible

The authors who skip proof copies almost always regret it. Some have had to pull books from distribution and start over.

Why Publishing Without a Proof is a Costly Mistake

Some authors convince themselves they can skip the proof stage to save time or money. They hit publish based on a PDF preview alone, trusting that everything will translate perfectly to print. It won't. Digital previews cannot show real-world issues like trim shifts, spine misalignment, color distortion, or paper transparency. Publishing without ordering and physically reviewing a proof is gambling with your reputation. It's far better to discover flaws privately than to let your

DO NOT SKIP PROFESSIONAL PROOF COPIES

paying readers find them publicly—and leave reviews that you can't erase. One small mistake on a proof can be fixed. Once it's live and sold, that mistake lives forever.

You've already poured months or years into writing your book. Don't sabotage yourself by rushing the final, critical step. Order that proof copy. Hold your book. Make it right before your readers do.

DO NOT CHOOSE ODD TRIM SIZES

Size Matters: Why Book Dimensions Make or Break Your Success

The size of your book isn't just a minor design choice—it's a critical business decision. Get it wrong, and it could cost you readers, sales, and credibility.

Most authors don't even think about trim size until it's too late. They focus on the cover, the formatting, the interior design—but they skip the conversation about dimensions, assuming it's a small detail. It's not.

Your trim size controls everything:

- Production costs and pricing
- Printing options and paper requirements
- Shelf placement in bookstores
- Reader comfort and experience

- Perceived value and professionalism
- Distribution possibilities
- Shipping costs

The Fastest Way to Look Unprofessional

I've seen it happen hundreds of times. Authors, wanting to be "creative," pick odd trim sizes that don't fit the style or genre. Instead, they destroy their own product.

That unusual trim size? It costs more to print. It doesn't fit standard bookstore shelving. It feels awkward in the reader's hands. And it screams, "This is a self-published book by someone who didn't do their homework."

Reality check: In publishing, "creative" sizing almost always translates to "difficult and unprofessional." Readers don't want books that are hard to hold. Bookstores don't want books that don't fit shelves. Printers charge more for odd sizes. Every decision you make affects the entire ecosystem your book needs to survive in.

The Bad Choices Authors Make

Here's where authors go wrong most often:

- Choosing square books for novels (expensive to print, awkward to hold)
- Selecting oversized dimensions for short manuscripts (makes the book look thin and flimsy)
- Using tiny trim sizes to make short books appear thicker (makes text cramped)

- Creating custom dimensions that don't match genre standards
- Choosing large trim sizes to reduce page count (backfires on printing costs)
- Selecting impractical trim sizes that don't fit standard shipping packages

None of these choices help you sell more books. They make your book harder to print, harder to sell, and harder for readers to enjoy. Your goal isn't to stand out for the wrong reasons. Your goal is to meet expectations so readers focus on your words—not struggle with your packaging.

Standard Trim Sizes that Work

These aren't arbitrary recommendations. These are industry standards that evolved because they deliver the best experience across genres:

- Fiction: 5.5" x 8.5" or 5" x 8" (most common)
- Literary fiction: 5.25" x 8" (elegant proportions)
- Trade nonfiction: 6" x 9" (professional standard)
- Textbooks/reference: 7" x 10" (allows for graphs/illustrations)
- Children's picture books: 8" x 10" or 8.5" x 8.5"
- Poetry: 5.5" x 8.5" or 6" x 9" (traditional formats)
- Memoir: 5.5" x 8.5" (familiar and comfortable)

If you stay within these standards, your book will feel right to readers, cost less to produce, and fit into the existing retail system without friction. Outside these ranges? Expect printing costs to spike, shipping to become a problem, and bookstore interest to vanish.

Before You Choose, Ask These Questions:

- What are the top 20 books in my genre, and what sizes are they?
- How will this size impact my printing costs and final retail price?
- Will this size work with standard POD (print-on-demand) services?
- Does this size accommodate my word count without looking too thin?
- Will readers find this size comfortable to hold and read?
- Does this size allow for proper margins and font sizing?
- Will bookstores be able to shelve this size normally?

The wrong trim size doesn't just look bad—it costs you real money. Bigger books require bigger shipping fees. Custom sizes often block you from expanded distribution. Overpriced books drive readers away. Weird sizes cause readers to doubt your professionalism before they even open your book. Every mistake here becomes a silent reason someone chooses another book instead of yours.

DO NOT CHOOSE ODD TRIM SIZES

Shrinking and Stretching Won't Save You

Authors with short manuscripts often try to "fix" it by shrinking the trim size or jamming the text tighter. Bad move. Shrinking margins, tightening line spacing, or reducing font size to stretch your content doesn't make your book better—it makes it harder to read. It makes you look like you didn't know what you were doing.

The same goes for bloating your trim size to make a book seem "more important." You'll just raise production costs, force yourself to price the book higher, and lose buyers who don't want to pay extra.

The Physical Reality You Can't Ignore

When a reader picks up a book, the first impressions matter. If the book feels odd in their hands, they're already questioning the quality before they read a single word. If bookstores can't shelve it properly, they won't stock it. If online retailers have to list it at a strange price point because of printing costs, you'll get undercut by competitors using smarter standard sizes.

Publishing a book is about making it easy for people to buy, hold, read, and recommend. The wrong size fights against you at every step.

The right trim size becomes invisible. It fits the reader's hands. It fits their expectations. It fits the shelf. It fits the price they're willing to pay.

The wrong size sticks out—and not in a good way.

Don't sacrifice your book's success because you didn't plan your dimensions like a professional. Pick a size that works. Respect the standards that exist. Give your book its best chance to succeed—starting with how it feels before a single page is turned.

DO NOT USE UNLICENSED STOCK IMAGES

Your book cover isn't just decoration—it's your first and most important sales pitch. When readers scroll through thousands of options, your cover decides whether they stop—or keep scrolling. Slapping some random Google image on your book is the fastest way to kill your publishing dreams before they start.

I've seen the aftermath firsthand. An author finds their "perfect" image online, slaps it on their cover, publishes proudly—then wakes up to a cease-and-desist letter. Or worse: Amazon yanks their entire book down without warning. All their reviews, all their rankings—gone. No second chances. No appeals.

That "free" image you found? Someone created it. Someone owns it. And that someone has rights you can't override just because the image showed up in a search.

The Real Cost of "Free" Images

When you use images without proper licensing, you're playing Russian roulette with your publishing career:

The internet made it easy to find images, but it didn't change copyright laws. That illusion of "free access" is a trap that has crushed more new authors than bad writing ever could.

How to Protect Yourself

What to Absolutely Avoid

I've worked with two authors that lost everything they built because they failed to take my advice.

The momentum lost when your book vanishes from retailers can destroy your sales for good. The financial blow from copyright infringement lawsuits makes properly licensed images look cheap in comparison.

Your words deserve legal protection. Your career demands it. Your readers expect a professional product.

Two outcomes. One: you invest wisely, choose a legal, professional image, and your book earns trust the second it hits the shelf. Two: you cut corners, grab a random image, and risk losing everything you built. It's not about luck—it's about decisions. Make the one that keeps your career safe.

DO NOT FORGET YOUR COPYRIGHT PAGE

The copyright page might seem like a small technical detail—but it's not. It's your legal shield, your public claim of ownership, and one of the most important pages in your entire book.

Skip it, and you're risking your rights, your royalties, and your reputation.

If you don't act like the owner of your work, don't expect anyone else to treat you like one.

What a Copyright Page Actually Does

A proper copyright page serves three powerful purposes:

Copyright exists automatically the moment you create original work. But a visible, professional copyright page shows that you understand and assert your rights—clearly and publicly.

Without it, you leave unnecessary gaps that opportunists and lawyers can exploit.

What to Include on Your Copyright Page

A standard copyright page doesn't have to be complicated. At minimum, it should include:

Here's a simple example:

> © 2025 by [Your Name] All rights reserved. No part of this publication may be reproduced, distributed, or transmitted in any form or by any means without the prior written permission of the publisher, except in the case of brief quotations embodied in critical reviews and certain other noncommercial uses permitted by copyright law. ISBN: [Your ISBN] Cover design by [Designer's Name] First Edition

That's it. Clean, clear, professional.

Why It Matters Even More for Self-Published Authors

When you traditionally publish, the publisher handles copyright documentation for you. When you self-publish, you are the publisher. That means it's on you to get it right.

A missing or poorly written copyright page tells the world: "This author didn't take their business seriously."

And in court—or in a marketplace flooded with scammers and idea thieves—sloppy or missing copyright documentation gives others an opening to steal, repackage, or claim your work.

Don't hand them that opportunity.

Protect your intellectual property properly. It's not optional. It's basic survival in this business.

Registration isn't required to own your rights, but it gives you stronger legal standing if you ever have to sue.

Skipping a copyright page is like building a house and forgetting to lock the doors.

It doesn't matter how great your content is. It doesn't matter how beautiful your cover looks. If you don't formally and professionally claim ownership, you make it easier for others to steal from you—and harder for yourself to defend what you built.

Take five minutes. Write the copyright page. Protect your book—and everything you worked for.

V. LEGAL & BUSINESS MISTAKES

DO NOT RISK YOUR WORK OR USE OTHERS' CONTENT ILLEGALLY

Protect Your Rights & Respect Others: The Legal Foundation of Your Author Career

Publishing a book means entering a world governed by copyright laws, trademark protections, and intellectual property rights. When you ignore these legal realities, you risk everything you've worked to build. This isn't about bureaucracy—it's about protecting your creative assets and respecting the rights of others.

Why Copyright Registration Matters

You spent months—maybe years—writing this book. Every word carefully chosen. Every idea carefully built. All that work deserves real protection.

Yes, under U.S. law, your work is automatically copyrighted the moment you create it. But there's a critical difference between having automatic copyright and having a registered copyright with the U.S. Copyright Office.

Without registration, your legal protection is weak at best. And if someone steals your work—and it happens more often than you think—you'll be facing an uphill battle to prove ownership, enforce your rights, and recover what you lost.

I've seen authors blindsided after discovering their books republished under someone else's name. In some cases, the thief had already registered the stolen material first—and was profiting from it. By the time the original author tried to fight back, it was too late.

The Power of Registration

The process to register your copyright is straightforward:

- Complete the application through the U.S. Copyright Office website
- Submit a copy of your work
- Pay the fee (currently $45-$65 for most single works)
- Wait for confirmation (typically 3-9 months)

This small investment gives you enormous protection. With registration in place, you can:

- Sue for copyright infringement in federal court
- Claim statutory damages (up to $150,000 per willful infringement)
- Recover attorney's fees if you win your case
- Create a public record of your ownership
- Establish a presumption of validity for your copyright

Without registration, you can only sue for actual damages, which are often difficult to prove and may be less than the cost of legal action.

Dangerous Myths About Using Others' Content

Just as you should protect your own work, you must respect others' rights. Many authors make dangerous assumptions about what they can freely use in their books.

Self-publishing doesn't mean you can take shortcuts with others' intellectual property. Copyright, trademarks, and intellectual property laws exist to protect creators—and violating them, even unintentionally, can lead to takedowns, lawsuits, and financial penalties.

Many authors assume that if something is available online, they can use it freely. That's not true. Every quote, image, font, or excerpt you use in your book must be legally cleared for commercial use.

What You Can and Cannot Use

You can't use copyrighted material without permission. Just because something is published doesn't mean it's free to use. Every book, song, image, and movie script is owned by someone, and unless that work is in the public domain, you need permission to use it.

What you can't use without permission:

- Extended quotes from books, articles, or interviews
- Song lyrics (even a single line)

- Images, photographs, or artwork
- Charts, graphs, or tables from other publications
- Characters or settings from other authors' works
- Modern Bible translations (like NIV or ESV)
- Trademarked brand names in your title or subtitle

What you can use freely:

- Facts, ideas, and concepts (not their specific expression)
- Works in the public domain (generally published before 1928)
- Your own original content
- Content used with explicit written permission
- Content covered by a license you've properly obtained

Fair Use Is Not a Free Pass

Don't assume "fair use" allows quoting anything. Many authors misunderstand fair use, believing they can quote any copyrighted work if they provide credit.

That is wrong.

Fair use is a legal defense, not a right, and it's only allowed under specific circumstances.

Fair use does NOT cover:

- Using substantial portions of works

- Using material that affects the market value of the original
- Using creative works just because you credit the source
- Commercial uses that compete with the original

Fair use MIGHT apply when:

- Using brief excerpts for legitimate commentary or criticism
- Creating parody that transforms the original
- Using small portions for educational purposes
- Transforming the material significantly for a different purpose

The Global Copyright Reality

International copyright is a maze most indie authors never navigate until it's too late. Your book can be stolen, copied, and sold by someone else in countries with weak enforcement—and you might have little recourse.

When you publish, your book receives automatic copyright protection in countries that honor the Berne Convention. But this isn't universal protection.

Some countries barely enforce copyright laws, creating safe havens for book piracy.

Let's clear up three dangerous myths right now:

1. Automatic copyright is NOT the same as registered copyright
2. The © symbol alone does NOT guarantee legal protection
3. International rights are NOT automatically enforceable everywhere

Protecting Yourself: The Action Plan

To safeguard your work and respect others' rights:

For Your Own Work:

- Register your copyright before or immediately after publication
- Include proper copyright notices in your book
- Monitor online for unauthorized uses
- Document your creative process and ownership
- Consider registering in major international markets

When Using Others' Content:

- Obtain written permission for any copyrighted material
- License images properly from reputable sources
- Keep detailed records of all permissions and licenses
- Verify public domain status before using older works
- Consult legal resources when in doubt

The Cost of Cutting Legal Corners

I've watched authors lose thousands in potential sales because they didn't protect their rights. One romance writer found over twenty copies of her books circulating on piracy sites within a single week of publishing.

Even worse, authors who unknowingly used copyrighted content have faced takedowns, lawsuits, reputation damage, and substantial legal fees. Some have been forced to pulp entire print runs, redesign covers, or withdraw books from distribution entirely.

Your creative work deserves protection. Other creators' work deserves respect. Building a sustainable publishing career means taking both responsibilities seriously.

The investment in proper copyright registration and legal compliance isn't just a cost—it's career insurance. It protects your ability to profit from your work, defend against theft, and build your business on a solid legal foundation.

Don't wait until you're searching for answers after the damage is done. Register your copyright now. Obtain proper permissions and licenses. Respect intellectual property boundaries. Your future income depends on it.

The path to publishing success contains enough challenges without adding legal troubles. Protect what's yours and respect what isn't—your publishing career will thank you.

DO NOT IGNORE TAX IMPLICATIONS

Taxes Aren't Optional – How Authors Must Handle Their Book Income

When you transition from writing as a hobby to earning income from your books, you step into the role of a business owner. That means taxes are no longer optional, and how you handle them can either protect or damage everything you're working to build.

Yet too many authors mistakenly believe they can quietly avoid reporting their book earnings—or they simply don't understand the rules. Both mindsets lead directly to audits, fines, interest penalties, and potential legal trouble.

Every platform you sell through reports your earnings to the government. Amazon KDP, IngramSpark, Draft2Digital, Barnes & Noble Press, Apple Books—all of them send income information to tax authorities like the IRS (United States), HMRC (United Kingdom), CRA (Canada), and others.

If you fail to report your author income correctly, it's only a matter of time before mismatched records trigger a closer look—and a potential audit.

No income is considered "too small" to matter once you meet these thresholds. Not reporting even a few hundred dollars can cost you much more later.

What Counts as Income for Authors

You are required to report:

- Royalties from book sales (print, ebook, audiobook)
- Advances from publishers
- Speaking fees related to your books
- Course or teaching income based on your expertise
- Crowdfunding contributions for your writing projects
- Merchandise sales related to your books
- Payments for articles, blog posts, or other writing
- Prize money from writing contests
- Tips or donations from readers
- Affiliate income from book-related recommendations

If you receive money because of your book or your expertise as an author, it's taxable income.

The Advantage You Have: Business Deductions

The good news is that running your author business allows

you to legally deduct legitimate expenses. Qualified deductions can significantly lower your taxable income.

Typical deductible expenses include:

- Professional editing, cover design, and formatting
- Marketing and advertising costs
- Website hosting and maintenance
- Professional memberships and subscriptions
- Research materials and reference books
- Office supplies and equipment
- Conferences and continuing education
- Travel related to book research or promotion
- Home office expenses (if you qualify)
- Software and services used for your writing business
- Professional services (legal, accounting, coaching)
- Publishing platform fees and commissions

Important: To claim deductions, you must have accurate, detailed records and receipts. If you cannot document an expense, you cannot defend it in case of an audit.

How to Keep Your Financials in Order

From day one, you should:

- Create separate business accounts for your author income and expenses
- Track every dollar earned and spent using accounting software or detailed spreadsheets

- Save receipts (digital or physical) for all business purchases
- Record business mileage and travel expenses as they occur
- Set aside a percentage of each payment for taxes (25-30% is recommended)
- Consider working with a tax professional familiar with creative businesses
- Learn the specific tax rules for self-employed individuals in your country

Waiting until tax season to figure it all out invites chaos, missed deductions, and potential penalties.

Estimated Taxes: Don't Wait for April

If you expect to owe $1,000 or more in taxes when you file, **you are required to make quarterly estimated tax payments** in the U.S. (and similar rules apply in other countries).

Failing to pay quarterly taxes can trigger penalties and interest—even if you eventually pay the full amount at the end of the year.

Plan ahead. Talk to a tax professional if you're unsure how much you should be paying quarterly.

Common Mistakes to Avoid

- Mixing personal and business finances

- Failing to report cash payments or direct reader contributions
- Claiming personal expenses as business deductions
- Missing quarterly tax payment deadlines
- Ignoring international tax implications of global book sales
- Failing to collect proper documentation for business expenses
- Not keeping up with changing tax laws affecting authors
- Assuming hobby status when you're actually running a business
- Neglecting to file the proper business entity paperwork
- Forgetting about self-employment taxes (in addition to income tax)

Taxes are not optional. But they don't have to be a nightmare if you manage them wisely from the beginning.

Quick Tax Survival Checklist for Authors

1. Register your business with appropriate local authorities
2. Obtain necessary business licenses and tax ID numbers
3. Set up separate business bank and payment accounts
4. Implement a reliable record-keeping system from day one
5. Schedule quarterly tax payment reminders

6. Budget for tax payments from each royalty deposit
7. Research specific deductions available in your country
8. Consider working with a tax professional experienced with authors
9. Keep business and personal expenses strictly separate
10. Document everything with proper receipts and records
11. Update your knowledge as tax laws change
12. File on time, every time—extensions to file don't extend payment deadlines

Remember: The goal isn't to avoid taxes—it's to pay exactly what you legally owe while taking advantage of all legitimate deductions available to you as a business owner. Proper tax management is part of building a sustainable, professional author career.

DO NOT IGNORE THE BUSINESS OF BEING AN AUTHOR

From Artistic Vision to Sustainable Success: Treating Your Publishing Like a Business

Behind every successful author stands a mountain of literary business knowledge that readers never see. It lurks beneath the surface of every brilliant sentence, every captivating character, every plot twist. The published book represents merely the creative tip of a massive business iceberg.

Yet too many authors crash against this hidden reality, refusing to see themselves as business owners until it's too late.

The Shift from Artist to Entrepreneur

I didn't fully understand that I was a business owner until I received my first significant royalty check. The reality hit hard: this wasn't just my passion anymore—it was commerce. If you're making money from your books, congratulations—

you're running a business, whether you've accepted it yet or not.

The transition often blindsides authors. Maybe it hits when your first Amazon payment lands in your account—or when someone asks for your business card at a signing event. That's when you realize art and commerce have merged, and new requirements now come with your creative work.

The Legal Foundation: Why You Need a Business Entity

If you're consistently selling books, you need to legally register your author business. Not doing so exposes you to tax issues, legal vulnerabilities, and lost financial opportunities.

Registering your business unlocks tax advantages you can't access as a hobbyist. Those deductions—home office expenses, conference travel, professional development, marketing costs—can significantly reduce your taxable income. What looks like modest profits at first can translate into real financial savings when handled correctly.

As your audience grows, legal protection becomes essential. A Limited Liability Company (LLC) shields your personal assets if someone sues you. Think it can't happen? Memoir writers have been sued for defamation. Non-fiction authors have faced legal claims over advice that allegedly caused injury. Without a business entity in place, your personal savings, home, and property are fully exposed.

Credibility also matters. A registered business allows you to open a business bank account, which elevates your professional image when accepting speaking fees, handling direct sales, or working with vendors. It creates a necessary separation between your personal and professional finances—something serious partners expect.

The Cost of Doing Nothing

Many authors continue operating as individuals without registration. While that might work at the hobby level, it creates serious problems as you scale:

- **Limited tax deductions** reduce your profit margins significantly

- **Personal liability exposure** puts your home, savings, and assets at risk

- **Commingled finances** create accounting nightmares at tax time

- **Unprofessional image** reduces opportunities with serious partners

- **Banking limitations** restrict payment options and financial tools

Your Business Structure Options

Sole Proprietorship: The default structure if you operate under your legal name. You report your book income on your personal tax return. Simple setup, but it offers **zero liability protection**.

DBA ("Doing Business As"): If you use a pen name and want to open bank accounts or sign contracts under that name, you may need to file for a DBA. It's still a sole proprietorship for tax purposes—it's not a separate legal entity.

LLC (Limited Liability Company): Creates a separate legal identity that protects your personal assets. Allows business tax filing, simplifies hiring contractors, and builds credibility. Ideal for authors earning consistent income who want to grow their brand safely.

S-Corp or Corporation: Advanced structures better suited for authors earning substantial income or expanding into broader businesses. They offer tax benefits but require more paperwork and formalities.

Understanding the Business Landscape

The resistance to learning the business side makes sense. Most of us enter this world because of our love for language or the urgent need to share ideas. We nurture our creative flames for years, protecting that flickering light against the winds of practicality. The suggestion that we must think like entrepreneurs feels like betrayal—a contamination of something pure.

This division—art versus commerce—is one of the most destructive myths in publishing. It's not a choice between craft or business. In today's landscape, business knowledge directly enables creative success.

Understanding publishing means recognizing the market structures and economic realities that determine which stories find audiences and which remain invisible. It means studying the financial foundations that allow authors to keep writing instead of abandoning their work due to economic necessity.

The Essential Business Areas Authors Must Master

1. **Production Economics**: Understanding printing costs, editing investments, cover design expenses, and marketing budgets transforms abstract creative ambitions into concrete business plans.
2. **Royalty Structures**: These numbers represent hours, days, and years of your life translated into financial terms. They determine whether writing remains a hobby or becomes a profession.
3. **Distribution Mechanics**: The relationships between publishers, wholesalers, retailers, and platforms create pathways that either carry your book to readers or leave it stranded in obscurity.
4. **Contract Management**: Understanding exclusive versus non-exclusive agreements, rights reversion clauses, and option provisions prevents costly mistakes that can haunt your career for decades.
5. **Financial Management**: Tracking income, planning for taxes, managing expenses, and budgeting for future projects are essential skills for sustaining your creative career.

Taking Action: Your Business Implementation Plan

1. **Register your business entity**—even a simple sole proprietorship with a DBA is better than nothing

2. **Open a dedicated business bank account** to separate personal and professional finances
3. **Create a basic accounting system** for tracking income, expenses, and tax obligations
4. **Establish professional business relationships** with contractors like editors and designers
5. **Set pricing and revenue goals** based on production costs and market realities
6. **Develop a continuous learning practice** to stay current with industry changes

Never Stop Learning: The Market Changes While You Sleep

Self-publishing today is not what it was five years ago—and five years from now, it will be unrecognizable again. Authors who stop learning get left behind. The ones who stay informed sell more books, reach more readers, and build sustainable careers, while the rest struggle to understand why their sales have dried up.

The most successful authors integrate business awareness into their creative process without allowing it to dominate artistic decisions. They understand market realities without becoming enslaved to them. They develop business strategies that serve their creative vision rather than replacing it.

The Choice Is Yours

Business knowledge is power—the power to sustain your writing life, to reach your intended readers, to build a career with longevity. It transforms publishing from mysterious lottery to strategic endeavor. It converts wishful thinking into purposeful action.

Your words deserve readers. Your creativity deserves sustainability. Your vision deserves effective execution. Business knowledge doesn't diminish these artistic values—it creates the foundation that allows them to flourish.

The choice was never between art and commerce. The true choice lies between navigating publishing blindfolded or with open eyes, between hoping for success or strategically building it, between surrendering to chance or claiming the power that comes from understanding the business reality surrounding your creative work.

Choose knowledge. Choose power. Choose the path that gives your creativity its best chance to thrive.

DO NOT IGNORE PIRACY

Protecting Your Book from Piracy: What Every Author Must Know

If you've published a book, someone is probably stealing it right now. Not tomorrow. Not eventually. Right now.

Most authors either don't realize their work is being pirated or assume there's nothing they can do about it. Both assumptions are costly—and dangerous.

Piracy isn't just someone casually downloading a $4.99 ebook. It's an organized business where others profit off your hard work. While you're working to build an audience, pirates are building subscription services around stolen books—including yours.

How Your Book Gets Stolen

Your book can show up in unauthorized places faster than you might think:

- PDF conversion of your ebook files
- Screenshots of pages shared on social media
- "Free ebook" websites offering direct downloads
- Subscription services offering unlimited reading
- Telegram channels and Discord servers sharing files
- Torrent sites distributing complete catalogs
- Counterfeit print-on-demand editions

It's not a rare occurrence. Pirated copies often appear within days of a book's release.

Finding the Thieves

Every author should take basic monitoring steps:

- Set up Google Alerts for your book title and name + "PDF" or "free download"
- Regularly search for your book title + "free ebook" or "download"
- Check major piracy sites quarterly
- Monitor your sales data for unusual drops
- Review online marketplaces for unauthorized editions
- Use reverse image searches to find your cover being used elsewhere
- Listen to reader feedback about suspicious versions

Authors have discovered their novels republished under different names, with only minor details changed. Often, piracy is discovered only because readers report suspicious listings.

Fighting Back Works

The Digital Millennium Copyright Act (DMCA) gives you tools to remove stolen content. When you find your work being pirated:

1. Document the infringement with screenshots
2. Find the hosting company's DMCA contact information
3. Send a properly formatted takedown notice
4. Follow up if content isn't removed within a reasonable time
5. Escalate to the hosting provider if the site owner doesn't respond
6. Keep records of all communications and actions taken

Most major platforms and hosting companies respond quickly when you submit properly formatted takedown notices. Filing these requests consistently helps minimize the spread of stolen content.

When Someone Steals Your Amazon Listing

Discovering your book pirated on Amazon itself can be especially damaging. If you find a fraudulent version of your book:

1. Document all evidence of your original publication
2. Submit an infringement complaint through Amazon's reporting system
3. Contact KDP support directly with your documentation
4. Report the issue to Amazon customer service as well
5. If necessary, ask your readers to report suspicious listings
6. Consider involving your publisher or an attorney for persistent issues

It's smart to search for your title under "All Formats & Editions" regularly and check for any suspicious listings under different author names.

Automation Is Your Ally

Manually searching for pirated copies can consume enormous time. Several services help automate protection:

- DMCA.com offers monitoring and takedown services
- Blasty.co automatically finds and reports violations
- Digimarc provides digital watermarking for tracking
- PublishDrive includes piracy monitoring in its distribution services
- AuthorCatch identifies unauthorized distribution channels

These services often pay for themselves by preventing just a few significant thefts.

The Strategic Giveaway Approach

Providing controlled free access can significantly reduce piracy. Many readers pirate content because it's hard to access legally—not simply to avoid paying. Strategies that help:

- Free first book in a series
- Limited-time promotions
- Library availability
- Kindle Unlimited enrollment
- Permafree titles for building audience
- Reader magnets in exchange for mailing list signup
- Sample chapters on your website

When readers have easy, legitimate access, piracy pressures can drop noticeably.

Reality Check: What You Can and Can't Control

You can:

- Monitor major platforms and search results
- Issue takedown notices for clear violations
- Educate your readers about supporting authors
- Make your work easily available through legitimate channels
- Pursue legal action for substantial commercial theft

You cannot:

- Eliminate all piracy completely

- Control every file once it's been downloaded
- Stop determined individual sharers
- Prevent all international infringement
- Block every potential piracy channel

Focus your efforts where they make the most difference: visible platforms, search results, and major download sites.

Piracy vs. Legal Resale: Know the Difference

Not every secondary sale of your book is illegal. The first sale doctrine allows individuals who legally purchase a physical copy of your book to resell it without your permission. This is why used bookstores, eBay resales, and library book sales are legal.

What's legal:

- Selling used physical copies of your book
- Lending physical books to friends
- Library circulation of purchased copies
- Donation of purchased books
- Reselling advance reader copies (though frowned upon)

What's illegal:

- Reproducing and distributing digital copies
- Creating unauthorized derivative works
- Claiming authorship of your content
- Selling counterfeit physical copies

- Removing DRM to enable unauthorized sharing

Understanding the difference ensures you focus your enforcement efforts on true copyright infringement, not lawful resales.

Take Action Now

Piracy isn't just about losing sales—it's about losing control of your creative work. Poorly formatted stolen versions can damage your reputation with readers who don't realize they've purchased unauthorized copies.

Your intellectual property deserves active, consistent protection. Defending it isn't optional if you're serious about building a sustainable writing career.

Start monitoring today. Act when violations occur. Protect what you've worked so hard to create.

Your future income—and your professional reputation—depend on it.

DO NOT INVENT AUTHOR IDENTITIES WITHOUT RESEARCH

Operating under a pen name requires more than updating your social media bio. You must legally register your pseudonym through a Doing Business As (DBA) filing if you intend to:

- Receive payment in your pen name
- Open bank accounts for your author business
- Sign contracts as your pen name
- Protect your intellectual property rights
- Conduct business legally under that identity

DBA requirements vary by state or country. Some jurisdictions require formal registration, public notices, and fees; others are simpler. Regardless of process, skipping this step can leave you unable to collect payment, open accounts, or prove ownership of your earnings.

Trademark and Brand Protection

Before committing to a pen name, authors must verify that it doesn't already exist as a protected trademark or active brand. Failure to do this research can lead to costly legal disputes.

Before adopting any pen name:

- Search the U.S. Patent and Trademark Office database
- Run comprehensive web searches
- Check domain availability
- Verify social media username availability
- Consult with a trademark attorney if the name will be central to your brand

Choosing a pen name means building a brand. If someone else already owns the name—or something too close to it—you could face a cease-and-desist order after investing thousands into branding, covers, and marketing.

Tax and Financial Implications

The IRS (and other tax authorities worldwide) do not recognize creative identities. They care only about the legal entity responsible for earnings. All income earned under a pen name must be reported under your legal name, linked to your Social Security Number (SSN) or Employer Identification Number (EIN).

Even with a pen name, your publishing income must be handled correctly through legal business structures. This requires careful recordkeeping and financial separation between personal and professional transactions. Failing to maintain this structure can trigger audits, delayed payments, and major financial headaches.

The Privacy Paradox

Pen names offer only limited privacy in today's connected world. If true privacy is a primary concern:

- Register your copyright under your legal name or business entity
- Use a P.O. box for all official correspondence
- Create author-specific email accounts
- Consider forming an LLC to add a layer of separation
- Be cautious about author photos and public appearances
- Understand that domain registrations may reveal personal information

It only takes one slip—one tagged social media post, one friend casually mentioning your real name—for the separation to disappear. The internet never forgets.

Multiple Pen Names, Multiple Complications

Managing multiple pen names means:

- Separate branding for each identity
- Different marketing strategies
- Multiple social media accounts
- Distinct audience building efforts

- Complex bookkeeping systems
- Additional legal protections

This multiplies the workload exponentially. Authors who attempt to juggle several pen names without systems in place often experience burnout and fragmented brand growth. If you plan to write under multiple identities, treat each one as a full brand that demands consistent time, energy, and business structure.

Collaboration Complications

If you collaborate with co-authors, ghostwriters, or illustrators under your pen name, you need ironclad contracts in place. These agreements must clearly define:

- Who owns the intellectual property
- How the pen name can be used
- Payment structures and schedules
- Rights to future works in the series
- Confidentiality requirements
- Exit strategies for the partnership

Without these protections, you risk ownership disputes, delayed payments, and conflicts that can permanently damage your publishing business.

International Implications

Publishing digitally makes your work instantly available worldwide. However, copyright laws, trademark protections, and business regulations differ by country. A pen name

DO NOT INVENT AUTHOR IDENTITIES WITHOUT RESEARCH

properly protected in the United States may not have the same recognition or legal standing in Europe, Asia, or elsewhere.

Authors selling internationally must research how intellectual property rights and business registration requirements apply in each major market they target.

A pen name is not just a creative mask. It is a business entity with real legal, financial, and strategic obligations. If you choose to use a pen name:

- File proper DBA documentation
- Consult with a publishing attorney
- Create a clear business structure
- Maintain meticulous financial records
- Understand the tax implications
- Be strategic about privacy protection
- Register appropriate trademarks if building a significant brand

Invest the time to set it up correctly now. The identity you build—and the writing career you grow—deserve full legal protection.

DO NOT SKIP BUSINESS INSURANCE

Most authors never think about business insurance until they urgently need it. By then, it's too late—and the consequences are costly.

The moment you publish a book for public consumption, you enter a world filled with legal and financial risks. Publishing isn't just a creative pursuit—it's a business. And businesses require protection.

Real Risks Authors Face

Consider these very real scenarios:

- A reader claims your health advice caused physical harm
- Someone sues you for defamation based on a character in your novel

- Your laptop with three unpublished manuscripts is stolen
- A child is injured at your book signing event
- You're accused of copyright infringement for using a quote or image
- Your home office suffers water damage, destroying your inventory
- Someone claims your memoir violated their privacy
- Your publisher goes bankrupt, holding your royalties hostage

These aren't rare hypotheticals. They happen—and they happen to authors who believed they were "just writing books."

Publishing carries real exposure. If you don't have insurance in place, your personal assets—your savings, your home, your future royalties—could be at risk.

Types of Insurance Every Author Should Consider

Professional Liability Insurance (Errors and Omissions Insurance): Protects against claims that your content caused financial, emotional, or physical harm. Essential for non-fiction authors, especially those offering advice in health, finance, legal, or lifestyle topics.

Even a simple typo in a dosage recommendation, or misunderstood financial guidance, can lead to lawsuits. Without coverage, defending yourself—even against false claims—can cost tens of thousands of dollars.

General Liability Insurance: Covers accidents like someone tripping at your book signing, falling during an event, or injuries involving your promotional materials. Medical bills and legal fees from these incidents can escalate quickly.

Property Insurance: Protects physical business assets such as laptops, external drives, inventory, marketing displays, and software licenses. If your home is damaged or your equipment is stolen, personal insurance likely won't cover losses tied to your business.

Common Insurance Mistakes Authors Make

- Assuming homeowner's insurance covers business activities
- Waiting until after publishing to secure coverage
- Failing to disclose all business activities to insurers
- Underestimating inventory value when calculating coverage
- Neglecting to update policies as the business grows
- Choosing generic policies not tailored to publishing risks
- Overlooking digital asset protection (manuscripts, artwork, layouts)
- Not including event coverage for book tours and signings
- Misunderstanding policy exclusions and limitations

Insurance needs evolve as your author business expands. Review your policies annually—or whenever major changes occur.

Why Acting Early Matters

The best time to secure coverage is before you publish, before your first live event, and certainly before your first legal notice. Insurance generally will not cover incidents that happened before your policy was active.

Defending even baseless claims out-of-pocket can destroy your finances. Having insurance in place provides not only financial protection but critical peace of mind.

Finding an insurance agent who understands the publishing industry is key. Many companies now offer customized packages specifically designed for authors, freelancers, and creative professionals.

Your Work Deserves Protection

Writing is hard enough without the additional burden of worrying about lawsuits, accidents, and unforeseen disasters. Insurance provides the freedom to publish boldly, promote confidently, and grow sustainably.

Your books should become your legacy—not the reason for your financial downfall.

Protect your words. Protect your work. Protect your future.

Secure the right coverage today—because once problems arise, it's too late to wish you had.

DO NOT WORK WITHOUT CONTRACTS

One of the biggest mistakes self-published authors make is failing to fully understand the contracts they sign—or worse, agreeing to work without any contract at all. Many assume verbal agreements or informal conversations are enough. Others skim lengthy documents filled with legal language, eager to move forward. Both approaches create serious risk.

If you are paying someone to help with your book—or collaborating with anyone—you must protect your work, your income, and your future with clear, properly negotiated contracts.

Why Trust Without a Contract Fails

Relying on trust or verbal promises is not professional. Without a written agreement:

- You have no proof of what was agreed upon

- Deadlines remain undefined and unenforceable
- Payment terms become subject to interpretation
- Rights ownership becomes ambiguous
- Dispute resolution has no clear path
- Expectations differ between parties
- Future usage rights remain unclear

Contracts aren't just "paperwork"—they establish legally binding protections for both sides. Without one, you are exposed to misunderstandings, financial loss, and legal disputes.

Ask Questions. Your Rights Depend On It.

That contract sitting in your inbox isn't just administrative formality—it's your future. When an illustrator, co-author, or anthology editor sends you a document filled with complex terms, stop and ask questions before signing anything.

If you don't fully understand the rights you're agreeing to, what feels like a professional milestone today can become years of regret later.

Rights Are Your Publishing Currency

As an author, your rights are everything. They are the assets you create, own, license, and monetize. Your copyright grants you exclusive control over:

- Reproduction of your work
- Distribution and sales
- Public display or performance

- Creation of derivative works
- Translation into other languages
- Adaptation to other media

Every contract you sign defines how these rights are shared, licensed, or transferred. Approach every agreement with the seriousness that your creative ownership deserves.

Collaboration Contract Red Flags

Working With Visual Artists

Authors frequently hire cover designers, illustrators, or concept artists. Before signing:

- Clarify who owns the final artwork
- Define where and how you can use the images
- Specify whether you can modify the work later
- Establish if artist attribution is required
- Understand any time limitations on usage
- Determine if you need exclusive rights

Professional artists often license usage rights—not ownership. Make sure you understand the difference before proceeding.

Co-Author Arrangements

Co-authoring can create powerful partnerships—or bitter legal battles—if rights are not properly defined. A co-author contract must clearly specify:

- Copyright ownership percentages

- Revenue sharing formulas
- Decision-making authority
- Revision and update responsibilities
- Series continuation rights
- Dispute resolution procedures
- Exit strategies if the partnership dissolves

With ghostwriters, contracts must explicitly transfer all rights to you. Without clear assignment of copyright, disputes can arise long after publication.

Anthology Agreements

Anthologies are where new authors most commonly lose rights unknowingly. Protect yourself by ensuring:

- The contract specifies how long rights are granted
- You retain copyright to your contribution
- The agreement defines what happens if the anthology goes out of print
- You have the right to republish your work after a set period
- Your compensation terms are clearly outlined

Avoid any contract demanding "full rights in perpetuity" unless you fully understand and accept the consequences.

Watch for "Work Made For Hire" Clauses

A "work made for hire" agreement means the hiring party, not you, owns the copyright. If you agree to this, you lose all rights to the work—forever.

Always read carefully. If you intend to retain control, do not sign work-for-hire agreements without fully understanding their scope.

Platform Terms Are Contracts Too

When publishing collaborative work through KDP, IngramSpark, or any platform, review the terms:

- Rights requirements for multi-author works
- Exclusivity clauses and limitations
- Distribution restrictions
- Payment structure for collaborations
- Content ownership declarations

Your internal contract should match the platform's terms to avoid future conflicts.

Everything Is Negotiable

Contracts are not final until signed. You can—and should—negotiate terms that are unclear, unfair, or overly broad. Reasonable publishers, editors, and collaborators expect negotiations. If someone refuses to discuss changes, it's a warning sign about their professionalism.

Examples of reasonable negotiations:

- Limiting rights to specific territories or languages
- Adding reversion clauses if the work goes out of print
- Clarifying merchandising and adaptation rights
- Setting time limits on exclusive rights

- Defining clear payment schedules and conditions
- Adding kill fees if projects are canceled

Protecting your future income is worth the conversation.

Professional Review Is Worth Every Penny

If you do not fully understand a contract, consult an intellectual property attorney before signing. The small cost of professional review is far less than the financial and creative losses caused by bad contracts.

Investing in legal review protects your ownership, your ability to grow your career, and your control over the worlds and characters you build.

Best Practices for Contract Protection

- Get everything in writing—always
- Create a contract template for recurring collaborations
- Keep signed copies of all agreements
- Document all changes with written amendments
- Read every word before signing
- Define clear deadlines and deliverables
- Specify payment amounts and schedules
- Include confidentiality clauses when appropriate
- Outline the exact scope of work
- Detail rights ownership and transfer terms
- Include termination procedures

DO NOT WORK WITHOUT CONTRACTS

Publishing is a business. Contracts define your ownership, your rights, and your income. No creative project is too small to deserve full protection. No opportunity is so urgent that it justifies skipping a careful review.

You are the first and final line of defense for the work you create. Protect your rights. Guard your future. Understand every contract—before you sign.

DO NOT IGNORE PRIVACY REGULATIONS

Email marketing gives authors one of the most powerful tools to connect with readers— but it also opens the door to serious legal and financial risk when handled incorrectly.

Many self-published authors start building email lists without understanding the laws that govern data collection and communication. They assume privacy regulations are designed for large corporations, not small businesses or individual writers. This is a costly mistake.

The moment you collect even a single email address, you are legally responsible for protecting that data—and subject to the same laws that apply to global giants like Amazon and Google.

Ignorance will not shield you from enforcement. Fines for violations can easily reach five or six figures, even for small-scale authors.

Privacy Laws You Must Know

Several major regulations impact how authors must manage email lists:

• **GDPR (General Data Protection Regulation)**: Applies to anyone with EU subscribers, regardless of where you're based

• **CAN-SPAM Act**: U.S. law governing commercial email communications

• **CASL (Canadian Anti-Spam Legislation)**: Strict regulations for anyone emailing Canadian residents

• **CCPA/CPRA (California Consumer Privacy Act)**: Affects anyone with California subscribers

• **PECR (Privacy and Electronic Communications Regulations)**: UK-specific requirements

• **National and regional laws**: Many countries have their own email marketing regulations

Privacy laws are real, and enforcement is rising as regulators worldwide tighten their focus on personal data protection.

Core Requirements for Compliance

Meeting your legal obligations requires careful, intentional action:

• **Explicit consent**: Subscribers must actively opt in (pre-checked boxes are illegal in many jurisdictions)

• **Clear privacy policy**: Must explain what data you collect and how you use it

- **Visible unsubscribe option**: Every email must contain an easy way to opt out

- **Accurate sender information**: Your name and contact details must be legitimate

- **Secure data storage**: Protect subscriber information from breaches

- **Documentation**: Maintain records of when and how consent was obtained

- **Third-party compliance**: Ensure any services you use also follow regulations

Mistakes That Lead to Heavy Fines

Common mistakes that put authors at risk include:

- Buying email lists or adding people without permission
- Using deceptive subject lines or misleading content
- Hiding unsubscribe options or making them difficult to use
- Continuing to email people who have opted out
- Failing to honor data access or deletion requests
- Not updating privacy policies when practices change
- Sharing subscriber data without proper consent
- Using non-compliant sign-up forms at book events

Remember: your email service provider may offer compliance tools—but the final legal responsibility always rests with you.

How to Fix Mistakes Immediately

If your current practices aren't compliant, take action now:

- Audit your current list for proper consent documentation
- Re-permission subscribers who were added without clear consent
- Update all forms and landing pages to ensure explicit opt-in
- Create or revise your privacy policy to be comprehensive and clear
- Implement double opt-in for all new subscribers
- Remove non-responsive or bouncing addresses
- Train team members on compliance requirements
- Document your compliance process for future reference

A smaller, verified, legally compliant list is far more valuable than a large, legally vulnerable one. Protect yourself before fines, legal claims, or reputation damage occur.

Staying Compliant Long-Term

Privacy regulations continue to evolve worldwide. Staying compliant is not a one-time task—it requires ongoing vigilance:

- Schedule regular compliance reviews
- Subscribe to regulatory updates in your key markets

- Use reputable email service providers with strong compliance tools
- Verify third-party tools and plugins meet current standards
- Maintain clear records of consent for every subscriber
- Test sign-up processes regularly from different locations
- Stay informed about emerging privacy legislation
- Consider consulting with a privacy attorney annually

Your email list represents powerful direct access to readers, free from social media algorithm control. But with power comes responsibility.

Respect the privilege of entering someone's inbox. Follow privacy laws precisely. Protect your readers' trust—the foundation of your long-term success.

Cutting corners exposes your author brand to legal action, financial losses, and permanent reputational harm. A professional author treats email marketing with the same seriousness as publishing their books.

Your readers deserve better. And the law demands it.

DO NOT OVERLOOK SUBSIDIARY RIGHTS

Your book is not just a book. It is a property—an intellectual asset—with multiple revenue streams waiting to be tapped.

The words you crafted can evolve into audiobooks, foreign editions, film adaptations, stage plays, merchandise, and educational materials. These "subsidiary rights" often generate far more income over time than the original publication ever could.

Yet too many authors fixate solely on Amazon rankings or initial launch results, ignoring these broader—and often more lucrative—opportunities.

Selling your book is not the end of the story. It is only the beginning.

What You Actually Own

As the creator of your book, you automatically own a bundle of distinct rights, each of which can be separately licensed, sold, or retained:

- Print rights (hardcover, paperback, large print)
- Digital rights (ebook formats, apps, interactive versions)
- Audio rights (audiobooks, dramatizations, podcasts)
- Translation rights (by language, by territory)
- Adaptation rights (film, TV, stage, games)
- Merchandising rights (products based on your work)
- Serialization rights (excerpts in periodicals)
- Educational rights (course materials, study guides)
- Public performance rights (readings, theatrical presentations)
- Derivative works (sequels, prequels, related works)

As a self-published author, you begin with full ownership of all these rights. This level of control is powerful—but it also demands informed, strategic management.

Making Your Rights Work for You

Begin by creating an inventory of potential subsidiary rights for each book:

- Which rights have the strongest market potential?
- Which rights align with your personal goals and brand?

DO NOT OVERLOOK SUBSIDIARY RIGHTS

- Which rights can you exploit yourself vs. which require partners?
- Which rights should you retain for future opportunities?
- Which rights might generate immediate vs. long-term revenue?

When approached with rights offers—from audiobook producers, foreign publishers, or film scouts—proceed carefully:

- Research the market rate for similar rights deals
- Evaluate the partner's track record and reputation
- Clarify exactly which rights you're granting (and which you retain)
- Negotiate key terms beyond just financial compensation
- Consider the impact on other potential rights deals
- Secure reversion clauses if the rights aren't properly exploited

Audiobook Rights: You can produce independently through platforms like ACX or Findaway Voices, maintaining full control but covering production costs. Alternatively, you can license rights to an audiobook publisher, allowing them to handle production in exchange for a royalty share.

Translation Rights: International book fairs such as Frankfurt and London offer opportunities to connect directly with foreign publishers. Authors with strong domestic sales records often place foreign rights successfully through these channels.

Film and TV Rights: Understand that film options are not outright sales. An option gives a producer exclusive rights to adapt your work for a specific period (usually 12–18 months) for a fee. If the project moves forward, additional payments follow. Even expired options can provide valuable exposure and momentum.

The Ripple Effect of Rights Exploitation

Subsidiary rights deals amplify your reach:

- Each adaptation introduces your work to new audiences
- Foreign editions open entire new markets
- Film and TV adaptations drive book sales
- Merchandising creates additional revenue and visibility
- Educational adoptions build long-term, stable income
- Audiobooks capture readers who prefer listening to reading

Strategic rights management ensures your work lives in many forms, reaching diverse audiences while multiplying your income streams.

Successful independent authors treat rights not as afterthoughts, but as core business assets.

They:

DO NOT OVERLOOK SUBSIDIARY RIGHTS

- Track rights granted and retained for each title
- Include rights management in their business plans
- Network with potential rights buyers and partners
- Budget for professional contract review
- Stay informed about market rates and opportunities
- Recognize which rights deserve investment
- Know when to partner vs. when to produce in-house

Your book represents years of creative work. Its value extends beyond the pages you published. Every right attached to your story—audio, translation, film, stage, merchandise—offers a potential pathway to wider audiences and greater financial return.

Do not allow valuable opportunities to slip away through inattention or inexperience. Manage your rights strategically. Negotiate from a position of knowledge, not desperation.

Your story deserves every chance to succeed in every form it can take. And you deserve to retain control, benefit from your work, and ensure that your creative legacy is protected and profitable.

VI. PUBLISHING & DISTRIBUTION MISTAKES

DO NOT PRICE EMOTIONALLY

Your book is not just a book. It is a property—an intellectual asset—with multiple revenue streams waiting to be tapped.

The words you crafted can evolve into audiobooks, foreign editions, film adaptations, stage plays, merchandise, and educational materials. These "subsidiary rights" often generate far more income over time than the original publication ever could.

Yet too many authors fixate solely on Amazon rankings or initial launch results, ignoring these broader—and often more lucrative—opportunities.

Selling your book is not the end of the story. It is only the beginning.

What You Actually Own

As the creator of your book, you automatically own a bundle of distinct rights, each of which can be separately licensed, sold, or retained:

- Print rights (hardcover, paperback, large print)
- Digital rights (ebook formats, apps, interactive versions)
- Audio rights (audiobooks, dramatizations, podcasts)
- Translation rights (by language, by territory)
- Adaptation rights (film, TV, stage, games)
- Merchandising rights (products based on your work)
- Serialization rights (excerpts in periodicals)
- Educational rights (course materials, study guides)
- Public performance rights (readings, theatrical presentations)
- Derivative works (sequels, prequels, related works)

As a self-published author, you begin with full ownership of all these rights. This level of control is powerful—but it also demands informed, strategic management.

Making Your Rights Work for You

Begin by creating an inventory of potential subsidiary rights for each book:

- Which rights have the strongest market potential?
- Which rights align with your personal goals and brand?

- Which rights can you exploit yourself vs. which require partners?
- Which rights should you retain for future opportunities?
- Which rights might generate immediate vs. long-term revenue?

When approached with rights offers—from audiobook producers, foreign publishers, or film scouts—proceed carefully:

- Research the market rate for similar rights deals
- Evaluate the partner's track record and reputation
- Clarify exactly which rights you're granting (and which you retain)
- Negotiate key terms beyond just financial compensation
- Consider the impact on other potential rights deals
- Secure reversion clauses if the rights aren't properly exploited

Audiobook Rights: You can produce independently through platforms like ACX or Findaway Voices, maintaining full control but covering production costs. Alternatively, you can license rights to an audiobook publisher, allowing them to handle production in exchange for a royalty share.

Translation Rights: International book fairs such as Frankfurt and London offer opportunities to connect directly with foreign publishers. Authors with strong domestic sales records often place foreign rights successfully through these channels.

Film and TV Rights: Understand that film options are not outright sales. An option gives a producer exclusive rights to adapt your work for a specific period (usually 12–18 months) for a fee. If the project moves forward, additional payments follow. Even expired options can provide valuable exposure and momentum.

The Ripple Effect of Rights Exploitation

Subsidiary rights deals amplify your reach:

- Each adaptation introduces your work to new audiences
- Foreign editions open entire new markets
- Film and TV adaptations drive book sales
- Merchandising creates additional revenue and visibility
- Educational adoptions build long-term, stable income
- Audiobooks capture readers who prefer listening to reading

Strategic rights management ensures your work lives in many forms, reaching diverse audiences while multiplying your income streams.

Successful independent authors treat rights not as afterthoughts, but as core business assets.

They:

- Track rights granted and retained for each title
- Include rights management in their business plans
- Network with potential rights buyers and partners
- Budget for professional contract review
- Stay informed about market rates and opportunities
- Recognize which rights deserve investment
- Know when to partner vs. when to produce in-house

Your book represents years of creative work. Its value extends beyond the pages you published. Every right attached to your story—audio, translation, film, stage, merchandise—offers a potential pathway to wider audiences and greater financial return.

Do not allow valuable opportunities to slip away through inattention or inexperience. Manage your rights strategically. Negotiate from a position of knowledge, not desperation.

Your story deserves every chance to succeed in every form it can take. And you deserve to retain control, benefit from your work, and ensure that your creative legacy is protected and profitable.

DO NOT ACCEPT FREE ISBNS BLINDLY

An ISBN isn't just a random number. It's your book's DNA—the identifier that publishers, bookstores, libraries, and distributors use to immediately assess your publishing status.

Choosing a "free ISBN" from Amazon, Draft2Digital, or another platform seems like an easy way to save money. Many new authors take that option without hesitation.

But that small decision carries consequences that can quietly limit your book's potential long after publication.

What Happens When You Accept a Free ISBN

When you accept a free ISBN, you are not listed as the publisher. The issuing platform—Amazon, Draft2Digital, or another service—becomes the official publisher of record.

This creates several invisible barriers:

- Bookstores frequently refuse to stock books with Amazon-issued ISBNs
- Libraries often skip titles not published by recognized publishers
- Distribution options become limited to the platform that provided the ISBN
- Professional review outlets may automatically reject your submission
- Your publishing brand never builds industry recognition
- Moving your book to another platform becomes complicated

It's not about the quality of your writing. It's about the signal your ISBN sends to the industry: *Amateur. Retailer-dependent. Limited reach.*

What a Free ISBN Really Costs

While the upfront cost is zero, the hidden price includes:

- Reduced bookstore placement opportunities
- Limited library acquisition potential
- Complications when seeking foreign rights deals
- Difficulty establishing yourself as a legitimate publisher
- Restricted distribution options
- Less professional industry perception
- Logistical challenges if you need to change platforms

Accepting a free ISBN can quietly restrict your publishing options—often when you least expect it.

What Owning Your ISBN Unlocks

When you purchase your own ISBNs, you own your publishing identity. You are recognized as the official publisher, not a subsidiary of Amazon or any other platform.

Owning your ISBN provides:

- Complete control over where and how your book is distributed
- The flexibility to move between print-on-demand services
- Direct access to bookstore and library markets
- Professional recognition in industry databases
- The foundation for a legitimate publishing company
- Increased opportunities for foreign rights sales
- The ability to list your chosen business name as publisher

ISBN ownership isn't just about formality—it's about protecting your future.

But What If You Truly Can't Afford It Yet?

If purchasing an ISBN isn't financially possible at the start, it's okay to use a free ISBN temporarily. It's far better to publish and build momentum than to stall indefinitely waiting for perfection.

However:

- Plan to upgrade to your own ISBNs when financially feasible
- Consider purchasing ISBNs with your second or third book
- Recognize the limitations of free ISBNs from the beginning
- Budget for ISBN purchases as part of your long-term business plan
- Research options in your country (prices vary significantly by region)

Publishing is a marathon, not a sprint. Starting with a free ISBN doesn't lock you out of future success—but staying reliant on free tools forever can limit your growth.

The key is to approach ISBN decisions with full awareness, not by accident.

Choosing the Right ISBN Path for Your Goals

Your choice depends on your current goals and long-term vision:

- **If you're publishing primarily for family/friends:** A free ISBN is likely sufficient

- **If you want bookstore distribution:** Purchase your own ISBNs

- **If you're building a publishing business:** Invest in a block of ISBNs

- **If you're testing the market:** Start with free, but budget for ownership

- **If you're focused on multiple formats:** Prioritize ISBNs for print editions

Every format—paperback, hardcover, ebook, audiobook—requires a separate ISBN if you want full control across all channels.

Planning ahead protects your options before you need them.

Industry professionals check your ISBN before they check your cover. It tells a story about who controls your work—and how serious you are about your publishing future.

A free ISBN might save you money today. But in publishing, the cheapest choice often carries the highest hidden cost.

If you must use a free ISBN to start, do it with clear eyes. But build a plan to reclaim your full independence as soon as possible.

Own your work. Own your future. Own your ISBNs—because your publishing legacy deserves nothing less.

DO NOT PUBLISH IN ONE FORMAT ONLY

Publishing your book is only the first step. Getting it into readers' hands—and into every market possible—is where true success happens. Many talented authors release their book through a single platform, celebrate the launch, and then wonder why sales plateau quickly.

One platform is not enough and one country is not enough. Relying on a narrow distribution strategy closes critical doors:

- Bookstore placement opportunities
- Library acquisition channels
- International markets and audiences
- Alternative format revenue streams
- Protection against platform policy changes
- Direct reader relationships and data

A strong distribution plan multiplies your income sources, expands your reach, and protects your publishing business from market shifts. Your stories deserve more than limited exposure. They deserve a global audience.

Print Distribution Options

Print-on-Demand Services

- Amazon KDP Print (formerly CreateSpace)
- IngramSpark (connected to Ingram, the largest book distributor)
- Barnes & Noble Press
- Lulu
- BookBaby

Relying solely on print-on-demand distribution associated with a retailer severely limits your potential for bookstore sales.

Wholesale Distributors

- Ingram Content Group
- Baker & Taylor
- Cardinal Publishers Group
- Independent Publishers Group

Serious authors aiming for bookstore shelves and library catalogs must make their print editions available through wholesale distribution.

Direct-to-Consumer Sales

Selling directly through your website or a dedicated online storefront offers:

- Higher profit margins (no retailer commissions)
- Direct customer relationships and data
- Bundle opportunities (signed copies, merchandise)
- Special editions not available elsewhere
- Immediate revenue (no distribution delays)

Challenges: You manage printing, shipping, and customer service. However, strong direct sales channels often deliver the highest profit margins and brand loyalty.

Ebook Distribution

Exclusive Ebook Programs

- Amazon's KDP Select (requires 90-day exclusivity)
- Benefits: Enhanced visibility, promotional tools
- Drawbacks: Limited to a single platform's ecosystem

Exclusive programs can be beneficial for certain genres, but exclusivity concentrates your risk on a single platform's policies.

Wide Ebook Distribution

Wide distribution can be achieved through ebook aggregators or direct uploads to individual retailers:

- Aggregators: Draft2Digital, PublishDrive, Smashwords
- Direct uploads: Apple Books, Kobo, Google Play, Barnes & Noble

A wide ebook strategy provides more resilience, especially as global ebook sales grow in emerging markets.

Audiobook Distribution: The Untapped Opportunity

Audiobooks represent one of the fastest-growing segments in publishing. Ignoring this format leaves behind:

- Commuter listeners
- Multitasking readers
- Accessibility-focused audiences
- Premium pricing opportunities
- International markets with strong audio adoption

Production Strategy: Audiobooks require upfront investment but recoup costs quickly due to higher royalty rates per unit sold.

- ACX (Amazon/Audible)
- Findaway Voices (wide distribution)
- Author's Republic
- Lantern Audio

Library and Bookstore Distribution

Libraries and bookstores are essential sales channels.

Library Access:

Make your books available through systems used by public and academic libraries:

- OverDrive/Libby
- Hoopla
- Baker & Taylor
- Bibliotheca

Offer competitive lending and pricing terms aligned with industry expectations.

Bookstore Access:

- Provide returnable options and standard wholesale discounts
- Develop direct relationships with independent bookstores
- Offer consignment arrangements for in-person author events and signings

Authors who ignore libraries and bookstores leave sustainable, long-term income on the table.

Going Global: Your Book Belongs to the World

Too many authors think locally when the real opportunity is global. The United States represents less than 5% of the world's population. Even combining all English-speaking countries still leaves the majority of potential readers untapped.

Digital distribution has eliminated barriers that once limited international reach. Today, readers anywhere—from Berlin to São Paulo to Tokyo—can purchase your book instantly.

Authors who think globally expand their income dramatically:

- English-language sales in non-English countries
- Foreign language translations
- International rights licensing
- Global audiobook adoption
- Alternative format opportunities by region

Building an International Presence

Distribution Matters:

Use distributors and platforms that provide true international reach. Prioritize ebook and audiobook availability in major global markets.

Understand Royalties and Pricing:

International royalty rates vary. Set strategic pricing tailored to each country's economic realities—not just currency conversion. Adjust prices thoughtfully for affordability and profitability across different regions.

Handle Tax Requirements Properly:

Many countries withhold taxes on royalties. Authors who complete necessary tax forms (such as tax treaties or exemption certificates) retain more income globally.

Translations Unlock New Readers:

- Consider starting with high-potential languages like Spanish, German, Chinese, or French
- Explore translation partnerships, revenue shares, or direct hiring
- Research market preferences in target countries
- Be patient—building an audience in a new language takes time

Cultural Adaptation Matters:

Success internationally isn't just about changing language—it's about respecting cultural expectations:

- Cover designs often differ significantly between markets
- Marketing approaches vary by region
- Genre preferences shift across cultures
- Release timing may need adjustment for local holidays/seasons

International Audiobook Growth:

As smartphone usage accelerates globally, audiobook consumption increases even in regions where ebook sales are slower. Distributing audiobooks internationally unlocks loyal listening audiences.

Work with International Influencers:

Build relationships with foreign book bloggers, reviewers, and reader groups. Local voices create trust faster than foreign marketing campaigns.

Strategic Timing and Multi-Format Launches

Launching all formats—print, ebook, and audiobook—simultaneously maximizes impact. Alternatively, staggered releases across formats or countries can sustain attention longer. Both approaches work when aligned with your broader marketing strategy.

Plan not just one release—but a growth roadmap across platforms, formats, and territories.

The Global Distribution Mindset

Success in today's publishing world requires an expansive view. Top authors:

- Think in multiple formats simultaneously
- Develop contingency plans for market shifts
- Monitor international publishing trends
- Build relationships with global industry professionals
- Consider foreign rights as core revenue opportunities
- Maintain flexibility across platforms and distributors

Before finalizing your publishing plan, ask:

- Which markets am I neglecting?
- What formats am I missing?

- Where are my international readers?
- How vulnerable is my current strategy?
- What happens if my primary platform changes policies?

Global thinking transforms a book launch into a publishing career.

A World Ready for Your Stories

Your book deserves to travel farther than your immediate surroundings. Publishing through one platform or one country guarantees missed opportunities. Limiting your distribution is limiting your future.

The readers who need your story are everywhere. In bookstores. In libraries. Listening on their commute. Browsing from halfway around the world.

Smart distribution is not just about reaching readers—It's about building a real, sustainable publishing business with no borders.

Think bigger. Distribute smarter. Go global. The world is ready for your book.

DO NOT MISS PRE-ORDER OPPORTUNITIES

Pre-orders can be one of the most powerful sales accelerators in publishing—when used correctly.

However, setting up a pre-order before your manuscript is complete is a critical mistake. I learned this the hard way—twice—and ended up losing my privileges for a year.

Self-publishing platforms enforce strict deadlines for pre-order fulfillment. Failure to meet those deadlines results in penalties ranging from suspended pre-order privileges to account restrictions—and most damaging of all, broken trust with readers.

Always complete your final manuscript before initiating a pre-order. Publishing success demands credibility, reliability, and professionalism. Protect your reputation by ensuring you can deliver the moment readers are ready to support you.

Once your manuscript is complete, pre-orders become an essential tool for building anticipation, boosting launch-day sales, and maximizing visibility.

Why Pre-Orders Matter

Your book launch is not a single day—it is a campaign. Pre-orders allow you to generate momentum before release, ensuring your book doesn't simply appear unnoticed.

Each pre-order counts as a sale on your release day, creating a concentrated spike that can:

- Push your book onto bestseller lists
- Trigger retailer algorithms to increase visibility
- Attract attention from industry professionals
- Generate social proof for undecided readers
- Provide revenue before your official release

Every pre-order represents a reader who believes in your book enough to purchase before seeing final reviews. These early supporters become your launch team—your first reviewers, your first promoters, and your first wave of visibility.

The Algorithm Advantage

Sales velocity matters. Selling 500 books on launch day creates a stronger algorithmic impact than selling 20 copies daily for 25 days.

A successful pre-order campaign generates concentrated momentum that:

- Improves your ranking in search results
- Increases visibility in "New Release" categories
- Triggers recommendation algorithms
- Creates a foundation for sustained visibility
- Establishes social proof for new readers

This early surge establishes critical visibility that advertising dollars alone often cannot match.

How to Structure an Effective Pre-Order Campaign

Set the Right Timeline

Most major retailers allow pre-orders up to 90 days, with some platforms permitting up to a year. For most independent authors, **30–60 days** strikes the ideal balance: enough time to build anticipation without losing urgency.

Smart Pre-Order Pricing

Consider offering a special pre-order discount. This rewards early supporters and creates urgency by offering a benefit that disappears once the book officially launches.

Urgency drives action—without it, readers often delay decisions indefinitely.

Pre-Order Marketing Strategies

Building successful pre-orders requires strategic, sustained effort:

- Create a dedicated landing page with sample chapters
- Design shareable graphics announcing the pre-order

- Email your list with exclusive pre-order bonuses
- Share the cover reveal to generate excitement
- Release teaser content throughout the pre-order period
- Host online events counting down to launch day
- Leverage partnerships with other authors
- Engage consistently on social media

Pre-orders are not something you announce once and forget. Successful campaigns require consistent updates, fresh content, and genuine excitement.

Strategic Benefits Beyond Day-One Sales

Pre-orders offer critical real-time feedback:

- Gauge reader interest before full release
- Test marketing messages and adjust as needed
- Identify potential launch problems early
- Build a list of engaged readers for future releases
- Fine-tune your release strategy based on pre-order data

Strong pre-order performance can also inform investment decisions, guiding where to allocate advertising and promotional budgets.

Even modest pre-order success enhances your credibility during outreach to media outlets, influencers, and retailers.

Post-Launch: Activate Your Pre-Order Supporters

Once your book is live:

- Thank pre-order purchasers personally
- Provide easy review instructions
- Offer shareable graphics and sample content
- Create a community around early readers
- Acknowledge their support publicly

Early reviews are critical for sustained visibility and reader trust. Your pre-order buyers are already invested—guide them naturally into becoming your first wave of advocates.

Publishing Smart with Pre-Orders

Used correctly, pre-orders transform a launch from a quiet release into a momentum-building campaign. They create urgency, maximize visibility, and provide crucial early support from your most loyal readers.

Respect your readers by delivering finished, polished work on time. Leverage pre-orders strategically to accelerate your growth, expand your audience, and position your book for lasting success.

Pre-orders are not simply an optional marketing tool. They are a smart publishing strategy for authors serious about building sustainable, credible careers.

DO NOT RUSH TO PUBLISH

There is a dangerous urgency that strikes near the finish line of any book project. After months—or years—of writing, editing, and planning, impatience can overwhelm even the most disciplined authors.

The temptation to publish immediately is powerful. The idea of holding a finished book in your hands—or seeing it available for purchase—becomes intoxicating.

But rushing your release undermines everything you have worked for.

Readers Only See the Final Product

Readers do not experience your timeline, your obstacles, or your personal investment. They encounter only the final product—and they judge it mercilessly if it feels incomplete.

A rushed book reveals itself through:

- Formatting inconsistencies
- Proofreading errors
- Substandard cover design
- Missing or incomplete front/back matter
- Incomplete metadata
- Poor category selection
- Weak book descriptions
- Unprofessional author bio

Every flaw sends the same unspoken message: *"This author did not respect their readers enough to deliver quality."*

In today's publishing landscape, where readers have endless alternatives, first impressions are irreversible.

The Hidden Costs of Rushing

A rushed launch damages more than one book—it damages your credibility:

- Negative reviews follow your book permanently
- Sales momentum becomes difficult to rebuild
- Marketing efforts yield diminishing returns
- Promotional opportunities with influencers vanish
- Your professional reputation suffers
- Reader trust, once broken, is nearly impossible to restore
- Future books start at a disadvantage

The market will not remember why you rushed. It will remember the unfinished product you delivered.

Proper Preparation Is Non-Negotiable

Successful books demand careful, professional preparation:

- Multiple editing rounds (developmental, line, copy)
- Professional proofreading
- Strategic metadata development
- Quality cover design
- Properly formatted front and back matter
- Optimized book description
- Strategic promotional planning
- Pre-release reviewer outreach
- Launch timeline development
- Consistent platform building

Every one of these steps demands time, focus, and investment. Skipping any creates visible gaps that readers will not forgive.

Examine the Real Motivation Behind the Rush

When the urge to publish prematurely strikes, step back and ask:

- Is this about reader benefit or personal impatience?
- Am I rushing to meet an arbitrary deadline?
- Will this book represent my best work?
- Have I completed every necessary production step?
- Is my marketing foundation established?
- Would I be proud of this version a year from now?

None of these reasons justify releasing work that is not truly ready.

Publishing is not the finish line—it is the starting gate. What you release must represent your best work, not simply your finished draft.

Protect Your Launch

Your initial launch window—when algorithms give you the highest exposure, when your marketing efforts peak, and when early readers are most engaged—is irreplaceable.

A weak launch wastes this momentum. A strong launch maximizes it.

Investing additional time now:

- Protects your book's critical first impression
- Ensures higher quality reviews
- Increases word-of-mouth potential
- Maximizes algorithm visibility
- Establishes your professional reputation
- Creates stronger reader relationships
- Builds confidence for future marketing efforts

Publishing too soon trades a fleeting feeling of accomplishment for long-term consequences.

Professional Standards Create Professional Careers

The authors succeeding in today's competitive marketplace are not necessarily the most talented. They are the most disciplined.

They:

- Respect production timelines
- Invest in professional assistance
- Prioritize quality over convenience
- Focus on reader experience above all else
- Build sustainable careers by protecting each release
- Understand that publishing is a marathon, not a sprint
- Never confuse finishing a manuscript with finishing a book

They refuse to settle for "good enough" when excellence is achievable.

Talent matters. But execution and professionalism matter more.

Publishing Smart

Your book deserves the time and resources necessary to achieve its full potential. Your readers deserve a polished, professional product. Your future self deserves the pride of knowing you launched with excellence, not regret.

Patience is not wasted time. It is the foundation of sustainable success.

Finish properly. Polish thoroughly. Launch strategically.

TAKE SELF OUT OF SELF PUBLISHING

The time you invest today determines the legacy your book will build tomorrow.

DO NOT OVERLOOK BULK SALES

Most self-published authors focus exclusively on individual retail sales—while overlooking one of the most lucrative opportunities in publishing: bulk orders.

One of my husband's colleagues found out I had written three children's books. He knew someone running a reading campaign, backed by a COVID-19 relief fund that supplied books to students. They asked for 120 copies for their second-grade classes. The students joined me on Zoom for a reading and Q&A session. Connecting with young readers and encouraging literacy during tough times was fantastic. I ordered the books, made a profit, sent an invoice, and arranged for direct shipment.

That single transaction moved more copies than months of individual Amazon sales—and it built relationships that opened even more doors.

Bulk sales transform your publishing business overnight. One organization ordering 100, 500, or 1,000 copies provides immediate revenue, expands your reach exponentially, and establishes your book in communities you would never reach through one-at-a-time retail sales.

The math is undeniable: Selling 500 books individually might take half a year or more. Securing one well-placed bulk order accomplishes the same result in a single deal—and without dependence on volatile algorithms or unpredictable online traffic.

Who's Buying Books by the Truckload?

Far more organizations need books than most authors realize:

- Schools and educational institutions
- Corporations for employee development
- Non-profit organizations and foundations
- Government agencies and programs
- Conference and event organizers
- Professional associations
- Libraries building specialized collections
- Faith-based organizations
- Health and wellness programs
- Military and veteran support services

Bulk sales extend beyond financial gain. They often lead to:

- Speaking engagements
- Workshop facilitation

- Consulting opportunities
- Media coverage
- Long-term organizational relationships
- Credibility with future buyers

Organizations that value your book often value your voice—and that creates new income streams beyond royalties.

Positioning Your Book for Organizational Buyers

Effective bulk selling begins with strategic positioning:

- Create a dedicated section on your website for organizational buyers
- Develop a one-page sell sheet highlighting organizational benefits
- Offer customization options (branded covers, custom forewords)
- Provide case studies showing successful implementations
- Create discussion guides or implementation materials
- Bundle complimentary resources with larger orders
- Offer virtual author visits with minimum order quantities
- Develop specific landing pages for different organizational types

Customization not only increases order size—it deepens the buyer's emotional investment.

Structuring Bulk Pricing

Bulk pricing must balance value for the buyer and profitability for you:

- 10-49 copies: 20-30% discount
- 50-99 copies: 30-40% discount
- 100-499 copies: 40-50% discount
- 500+ copies: Negotiable based on order specifics

Know your breakeven points in advance so you can negotiate confidently.

Fulfillment Tip: For significant bulk orders, consider professional fulfillment services to manage storage, packaging, and shipping.

Making Bulk Sales Happen

Bulk orders rarely happen passively. They require proactive outreach and relationship building:

- Research organizations aligned with your book's themes
- Identify decision-makers within target organizations
- Develop personalized outreach strategies
- Create sample packages for key prospects
- Attend industry events where potential buyers gather
- Partner with speakers/consultants who serve your target market
- Leverage existing readers who work in potential buying organizations

- Follow industry news for timely opportunities (new initiatives, funding)

Be patient: Bulk deals often involve multiple stakeholders and long decision cycles. An initial inquiry might take months to materialize into a signed deal—but the payoff is worth it.

Think creatively: Your novel about workplace dynamics might be ideal for corporate HR programs. Your memoir about overcoming adversity might resonate with non-profits supporting youth development.

Do not limit your thinking to obvious matches.

The Bigger Picture

Bulk buyers are not just customers. They become amplifiers of your brand, positioning your book—and your expertise—in front of hundreds or thousands of new readers simultaneously.

Each successful bulk sale strengthens your reputation, expands your platform, and builds sustainable business growth.

Not every book is an obvious fit for organizational sales, but many authors overlook incredible opportunities simply because they never positioned their books beyond individual readers.

Your book holds value not only for the single buyer browsing an online store—but for entire organizations seeking powerful, aligned resources to serve their communities, employees, clients, or students.

TAKE SELF OUT OF SELF PUBLISHING

Explore this hidden gold mine. One conversation could lead to your biggest sale yet.

DO NOT IGNORE SEASONAL TIMING

Timing matters.

Publishing your book the moment it's finished isn't a strategy—it's self-sabotage. The calendar directly impacts your book's visibility, sales potential, and longevity. Ignoring this reality costs you readers, revenue, and momentum.

Each month of the year carries specific advantages and challenges that will either boost your launch or bury it. Traditional publishers have leveraged this knowledge for decades, carefully selecting release dates to align with consumer behavior. As an independent author, you must adopt the same strategic mindset if you expect to compete—and win.

After guiding over 300 authors through the publication process, the pattern is clear: Those who plan their timing succeed. Those who publish impulsively often regret it.

Your book deserves better than random chance. It deserves intelligent, deliberate timing.

The Publishing Year Breakdown

January–February: Fresh Start Season

Ideal for self-improvement, health, business, and finance titles. Readers are motivated by resolutions but cautious with spending after the holidays. Nonfiction outperforms fiction during this window.

March–May: Spring Growth Cycle

Strong for literary fiction, memoirs, and practical nonfiction (gardening, lifestyle, education). Literary awards generate buzz, and academic institutions select fall course materials during this period.

Summer (Late May–August): Vacation Reading Season

Escapist fiction, thrillers, beach reads, and young adult novels thrive. Travel guides and children's titles gain momentum with school breaks and holiday planning.

Fall (September–Early November): Competitive Launch Season

Major publishers release their most anticipated titles. Media attention is high—but so is competition. Academic nonfiction, serious literary works, and award contenders perform exceptionally well.

Holiday Season (Mid-November–December): Peak Retail Sales

Giftable books dominate—coffee table editions, cookbooks, humor, and luxury versions. New releases must launch by mid-November to capitalize fully on holiday shopping patterns.

Strategic Timing Beyond Seasons

Holidays Create Natural Promotional Hooks:

- Align romance novels with Valentine's Day
- Launch parenting books near Mother's Day or Father's Day
- Release horror around Halloween
- Time financial guides for tax season
- Position inspirational titles near graduation season

Plan Backwards: If you want strong Valentine's Day sales for a romance novel, your launch should happen in late December or early January. If you want Halloween momentum for a horror collection, publish in August or early September to allow buzz to build.

Leverage Event Calendars:

- Industry conferences related to your topic
- Major cultural events aligned with your theme
- Relevant awareness months (e.g., Mental Health Awareness Month)
- Seasonal activities that connect with your content
- Historical anniversaries that tie to your subject matter

Avoid Dead Zones and Competitive Traffic Jams

Competitive Research Matters: Study upcoming release calendars for your genre. Avoid launching alongside a highly anticipated book that could dominate reader and media attention.

Beware Publishing Dead Zones:

- The week between Christmas and New Year's
- Major holiday weekends
- Mid-August (when media attention dwindles)
- Thanksgiving week
- April 15 (tax deadline in the U.S.)

Publishing during these dead zones often leads to weak launches and limited promotional opportunities.

Consider Personal Capacity: Align your release schedule with your personal calendar. Avoid launching during periods when professional, personal, or family obligations will prevent you from promoting effectively. Perfect market timing means nothing if you're too overwhelmed to capitalize on it.

Format and Pre-Order Considerations

Format Behavior Varies:

- Ebooks perform best with immediate availability
- Print sales align closely with seasonal patterns
- Audiobooks follow different consumption cycles
- Hardcovers benefit from holiday gift-giving windows

DO NOT IGNORE SEASONAL TIMING

- Special editions require longer promotional runways

Pre-Orders Build Momentum:

- 30-60 days is optimal for most titles
- Longer pre-order windows benefit established authors
- Short pre-orders (7-14 days) work for authors with engaged platforms
- Pre-order incentives increase conversion rates
- Strategic pre-order discounting can boost initial numbers

For Series Authors:
- Space releases 3-4 months apart for momentum
- Release companion novellas between major launches
- Time series box sets for peak sales periods
- Consider simultaneous format releases for each title
- Plan series completion to coincide with high-visibility seasons

The most successful self-published authors treat timing as a strategic asset—not an afterthought.

They:

- Analyze category and genre performance by season
- Study competitor release schedules
- Coordinate launches with natural promotional hooks
- Align publication with personal promotion capacity
- Build backwards from key retail opportunities

- Match formats with ideal seasonal windows
- Create multi-format launch strategies

Your book's timing determines whether it quietly disappears or explodes into a receptive market.

Publishing intelligently isn't just about writing a great book—it's about releasing it at the moment readers are most ready to embrace it.

Give your book the full advantage of professional timing. Your future sales, brand growth, and publishing success depend on it.

DO NOT FORGET SPECIAL EDITIONS

Most self-published authors stop at basic formats—paperbacks and ebooks—never exploring beyond them. In doing so, they leave significant money on the table and miss powerful opportunities to deepen loyalty among their most dedicated readers.

Creating premium or special editions isn't reserved for celebrity authors or major publishing houses. If you've built even a modest audience that values your work, you have every right—and every opportunity—to offer upgraded versions that readers will eagerly purchase. Often, these sales come in addition to your standard editions.

The model is simple: take your core content, enhance it meaningfully, and offer a higher-quality, more exclusive experience that justifies a higher price point.

Special editions not only increase revenue per reader—they forge stronger emotional bonds with your biggest supporters.

Why Premium Editions Matter

- Super-fans seek deeper connections with authors they love
- Collectors value uniqueness and limited availability
- Gift-givers look for special versions that demonstrate thoughtfulness
- Physical book buyers often appreciate tangible quality
- Premium formats create additional revenue streams from existing content
- Special editions extend the lifecycle of your backlist titles
- Direct sales of premium products build your independence from platforms

Ways to Create Valuable Special Editions

Hardcovers with Upgrades: A beautifully produced hardcover version immediately elevates your offering. Higher-quality binding, textured covers, and custom dust jackets create products readers want to display, gift, and cherish.

Signed and Numbered Editions: Personally signed copies—especially limited runs with hand-numbered editions—tap into readers' desire for exclusivity and collectibility.

Illustrated Editions: Incorporate original artwork, maps, photographs, or design elements that bring your world, story, or content to life visually.

Deluxe Slipcased Editions: Custom slipcases, embossed covers, ribbon bookmarks, or specialty paper transforms your book into a keepsake worthy of display.

Bonus Content Editions: Offer extended editions that include:

- Author commentary and annotations
- Deleted scenes or alternate endings
- Character interviews or "behind the scenes" content
- Research notes or source materials
- Extended appendices or glossaries

Bundled Collector's Sets: Package multiple books together in a themed set with cohesive design. Offer box sets for series, trilogies, or topical collections.

Personalized Editions: For ultra-premium buyers, offer customized editions where readers can:

- Have their name included in the acknowledgments
- Receive a personalized message on the title page
- Get a character named after them in future work
- Receive a custom letter alongside their book

Integrated Digital Bonuses: Enhance physical editions by offering private access to:

- Downloadable companion workbooks
- Video content accessible via QR codes
- Exclusive online communities
- Audio interviews or commentary
- Digital artwork or wallpapers

Limited "Author's Cut" Editions: Offer a special version available only through direct sales on your website, unavailable on third-party platforms, making your most loyal readers feel like true insiders.

Pricing Strategy for Premium Editions

Each premium tier must deliver unmistakable added value:

- Base edition: Standard paperback or ebook pricing
- Enhanced edition: 30-50% above base price
- Collector's edition: 100-200% above base price
- Ultimate/deluxe edition: 300%+ above base price
- Personalized limited editions: Custom pricing based on exclusivity

Readers are willing to pay for enhancements they perceive as authentic, meaningful, and special. However, attempting to charge a premium for an unchanged product erodes trust. Every upgraded edition must genuinely enrich the reader's experience.

Low-Budget Premium Options

Even on a limited budget, meaningful special editions are achievable:

- Hand-signed bookplates attached to standard editions
- Limited print runs with numbered certificates
- Custom bookmarks or reading companions
- Access to private online content or communities
- Personal thank-you notes included with purchases
- Bonus digital content delivered via email

Creativity and sincerity always outperform lavish production when budgets are tight.

Why This Matters

Premium editions do more than increase your revenue:

- They create deeper emotional connections with readers
- They provide marketing talking points and launch momentum
- They establish your work as collectible and valuable
- They help you build direct sales channels
- They give readers multiple ways to support your work
- They extend the lifecycle of your existing catalog
- They increase your perceived professionalism and status

Your words have value beyond the basic version. Special editions recognize that value—offering enhanced, upgraded experiences that deepen engagement and strengthen your author business.

Smart independent authors think beyond basic formats. They create ways for readers to invest even more fully—financially and emotionally—in their worlds, their messages, and their brands.

Build premium editions. Reward your most loyal fans. Grow your income—and your impact.

DO NOT WASTE SERIAL RIGHTS

One of the most overlooked opportunities in publishing is treating a book as if it exists only to be sold as a complete unit. That narrow thinking limits your reach—and leaves significant money on the table.

Your book isn't just a book. It's a collection of valuable content that can be repurposed, reshaped, and monetized multiple times over. Serial rights allow you to extract more revenue, generate targeted visibility, and build momentum long after your book's release.

Traditional publishers have leveraged serial rights for decades. It's time for independent authors to do the same.

First vs. Second Serial Rights

First Serial Rights involve selling excerpts of your book before its official release. This creates early buzz, introduces your work to new readers, and builds credibility through association with established media outlets. Payments for first rights can range from modest fees to substantial advances—especially from major publications.

Second Serial Rights come into play after publication, allowing you to excerpt content for new audiences without undermining book sales. Second rights extend your visibility well beyond the typical launch window, giving your book renewed life over time.

The promotional value alone often justifies these opportunities. A well-placed excerpt reaches pre-qualified audiences and drives readers back to your full book with far more efficiency than traditional advertising.

Strategic Content Repurposing

Serial rights success isn't about copy-pasting random chapters. It's about **thoughtfully adapting** your material for different audiences while preserving the core value of your work.

Examples:

- A business book chapter becomes a leadership article for Harvard Business Review
- A cookbook recipe collection transforms into seasonal food features
- A memoir's powerful scene works as a standalone personal essay
- A novel's opening creates intrigue as a literary magazine submission

- A self-help book's framework becomes a series of advice columns

For nonfiction authors: Serial rights establish you as an expert and open doors to speaking engagements, consulting, and broader media coverage.

For fiction authors: They build name recognition, strengthen your portfolio, and grow your audience organically.

Digital Expansion Opportunities

Today's serial rights opportunities extend far beyond traditional print:

- Online magazines and digital publications
- Industry newsletters with targeted audiences
- Podcast transcripts and companion content
- Popular blogs and content platforms
- Social media partnerships and sponsored content
- Email newsletters with engaged subscriber bases

Publication on respected digital platforms often delivers greater promotional impact than short-lived retail advertising—and offers the bonus of borrowed credibility from established brands.

Timing Your Serial Strategy

First Serial Placements: Target publication 4–8 weeks prior to your book's official launch. This builds anticipation without diluting urgency.

Second Serial Placements: Use during promotions, re-releases, related news events, or seasonal marketing pushes to revitalize interest in backlist titles.

Strategic serial placements maintain visibility long after your book's release date has passed.

Key Considerations When Licensing Serial Rights

- **Word count limits:** Typically 10-15% of your total book
- **Exclusivity periods:** Usually 30-90 days for first rights
- **Territorial restrictions:** North American, international, or language-specific
- **Attribution requirements:** Book title, publication date, publisher info
- **Compensation structure:** Flat fee vs. royalty percentage
- **Purchase link inclusion:** Direct readers back to your book
- **Author bio requirements:** Leverage the opportunity for platform building
- **Rights reversion timeline:** When control returns fully to you

Develop a Tiered Serial Rights Strategy

Build a three-level targeting system:

- **Tier 1:** Major publications with broad reach (national magazines, high-traffic websites)

- **Tier 2:** Industry-specific outlets with targeted audiences (trade journals, specialized blogs)
- **Tier 3:** Community-level publications (local newspapers, regional magazines)

Prepare a **Serial Rights Kit** including:

- 3-5 potential excerpts of varying lengths
- Suggested headlines and subheadings
- Brief contextual introductions
- Author bio and credentials
- High-resolution author photo
- Book cover image
- Sample interview questions
- Publication timeline and contact information

Having a professional package ready makes it easier to pitch and close opportunities quickly.

Serial Rights Are Only the Beginning

Serial rights are one category among many subsidiary rights opportunities. Others include:

- Foreign language rights
- Audio rights
- Film and television adaptation rights
- Merchandise and product licensing
- Educational and curriculum licensing
- Book club and special edition rights

Each right represents an additional revenue stream beyond traditional book sales.

Serial rights, however, offer a rare combination: immediate financial return and strategic audience building. They turn pieces of your existing work into income-generating, visibility-expanding tools without requiring full new products.

Your book's value extends far beyond the finished manuscript. Serial rights allow you to extract that value thoughtfully, maximizing both financial return and reader impact.

Treat your content like the asset it is—multi-dimensional, multi-use, and capable of opening doors long after publication day.

Smart authors don't just sell books. They create ecosystems around their content. Serial rights are one of the smartest places to start.

VII. MARKETING & PROMOTION MISTAKES

DO NOT WRITE GENERIC AUTHOR BIOS

Your author bio isn't filler. It's not optional. It's one of the first and most important chances you have to hook a reader outside your actual book. Whether someone finds you on Amazon, your website, a blog interview, or a podcast introduction—your bio speaks before you ever do.

And too many authors blow it.

They throw together a few sentences about loving coffee, living with their cat, and always dreaming of writing a book. Cute, but irrelevant. Readers aren't buying your love of caffeine. They're looking for a reason to trust you, connect with you, or believe that you're the one they should invest their time (and money) in.

If you can't sell yourself in 100 words or less, readers will doubt you can hold their attention for 300 pages. It's that simple.

Here's what a good bio actually does: it builds credibility, shows personality, reinforces your brand, and positions you exactly where you need to be in your readers' minds. It's strategic marketing—not autobiography.

If you write nonfiction, your bio has one job first: prove you're worth listening to. That means showing real expertise, not just saying you're "passionate" about a topic. Numbers, recognitions, achievements—specifics are what matter. If you helped 500 entrepreneurs double their revenue, say that. If you've been featured in industry magazines, mention it. Nobody cares about vague claims—they care about results and receipts.

If you write fiction, your bio has a different first job: connection. Readers want to know the mind behind the stories. That doesn't mean dumping random facts—it means showcasing your voice and hinting at what makes your storytelling different. Fiction bios should feel like an invitation, not a resume.

And whatever you write, remember: readers want a person, not a sales robot. That's why the best bios have carefully chosen personal touches. They hint at who you are only where it makes you more relatable, memorable, or aligned with your brand. Not every detail belongs. (Your three cats, your love of pineapple pizza, your obsession with sock collecting—mention it if and only if it helps people connect with your writing, your message, or your genre.)

Your bio also needs to match the platform. You don't get the same amount of space everywhere.

DO NOT WRITE GENERIC AUTHOR BIOS

Another mistake? Treating your bio like it's set in stone. It's not. You need to update it as you grow. New books, new awards, new directions—you're evolving, and your bio needs to keep pace with that.

If you want to make your bio powerful, follow these simple steps:

If you ignore your author bio, you're throwing away one of your best chances to turn browsers into readers—and readers into loyal fans. If you optimize it, update it, and make it work for you, your bio stops being background noise and starts being the first step toward building your author brand the right way.

DO NOT ASSUME BOOKS SELL THEMSELVES

Most self-published authors believe the myth that once you upload your book, readers will magically find it. They won't.

Publishing without marketing is opening a store in the middle of the desert and expecting customers. Your brilliant story doesn't matter if no one knows it exists.

Strong book launches happen because authors start marketing long before release day. When you wait until your book is available to start talking about it, you're already behind. You'll have zero momentum, no audience waiting, and no pre-release buzz.

Successful authors understand that effective book marketing begins the moment you commit to writing—sometimes even earlier. Your launch isn't the start of your marketing; it's the payoff for the audience you built in advance.

Start by identifying your ideal readers and discovering where they gather. Focus your energy on the platforms, communities, blogs, and podcasts where your readers already exist, rather than trying to be everywhere.

Share your writing journey—the wins, the struggles, the insights. Let readers feel part of the process. The more people connect with your personal journey, the more invested they become in your eventual success.

Build your email list from the beginning. Unlike social media where algorithms control reach, email marketing gives you direct access to readers who've chosen to hear from you. Offer something valuable in exchange for subscriptions—a free short story, exclusive content, or sample chapters.

Use Advance Reader Copies (ARCs) to generate early reviews and build momentum before your book even launches. Reviews create credibility, drive algorithm visibility, and help hesitant buyers trust that your book is worth their time.

Strategic partnerships with other authors in your genre can expand your reach exponentially. Cross-promotion allows you to tap into existing audiences that are already predisposed to like your work.

Pre-orders create urgency and maximize visibility on release day. Offering your book for pre-order allows you to stack early sales toward launch algorithms, making it easier to hit bestseller lists and recommendation engines.

Marketing is not about bombarding strangers with sales links. It's about building relationships. Readers don't buy books because you tell them to—they buy because they've connected with you.

The authors who fail are those who treat marketing as something to do after the writing is done. The authors who succeed start planting marketing seeds from day one.

Your book is invisible without marketing. Visibility requires consistent, strategic effort over time.

If you want readers to celebrate your launch, start giving them reasons to care now—not after you hit publish.

DO NOT SPAM READERS WITH BOOK LINKS

Nothing turns readers away faster than an author constantly yelling, "Buy my book!"

Too many authors think marketing means flooding every platform with sales links. Let me be blunt: nobody likes being sold to nonstop.

Spamming Destroys Your Reputation

When you treat every interaction like a sales pitch:

- Readers tune out your message completely
- Social media platforms flag your content as promotional
- Online communities begin to avoid you
- Potential readers develop negative associations with your name
- Industry professionals notice and distance themselves

- Your credibility as an author diminishes

The most effective book promotion happens when readers feel naturally drawn to you—not pressured.

Marketing That Actually Works

Instead of pushing your book on everyone, focus on attraction marketing. People buy from authors they know, like, and trust—in that order.

Be a Community Member First, Author Second

Before posting about your book in any group or forum:

- Spend time understanding the community culture
- Contribute valuable content and responses
- Build relationships through genuine engagement
- Establish yourself as a helpful resource
- Respect group rules about self-promotion
- Follow the 80/20 rule: 80% helpful content, 20% promotion

When I published my first book, I focused on helping others solve publishing challenges. My genuine contribution created curiosity about my work without ever spamming.

Create Content Worth Engaging With

Readers care about your book when they see value in what you share:

- Solve real problems related to your book's topic

- Share authentic stories from your writing journey
- Provide insights that showcase your expertise
- Start meaningful conversations around your themes
- Create shareable content that entertains or educates
- Develop a distinct voice that stands out naturally

If you've written a relationship book, spark discussions about communication styles. If it's fantasy, talk about worldbuilding challenges. Get readers thinking and talking.

Give Value Before Asking for the Sale

Before promoting your book:

- Offer valuable free content that demonstrates your expertise
- Create helpful resources related to your book's topic
- Build an engaged audience through consistent value
- Develop relationships with potential readers
- Establish credibility through quality content
- Understand what your audience truly needs

When I launched my self-publishing guide, I first offered a free checklist of common publishing mistakes. Readers who valued that checklist naturally wanted the full book.

Leverage Other People's Platforms

Don't do all the work yourself:

- Pursue podcast interviews related to your expertise
- Write guest posts for relevant blogs

- Participate in virtual events and conferences
- Collaborate with complementary authors
- Seek honest reviews from established reviewers
- Create valuable content partners can share

A recommendation from a third party carries ten times the weight of direct self-promotion.

Build and Respect Your Email List

An email list is your most valuable marketing asset because:

- You own the relationship directly
- Emails reach readers without algorithm interference
- Subscribers have actively chosen to hear from you
- Email marketing has higher conversion rates than social media
- You can segment and personalize your approach
- It's a direct channel to your most interested readers

Respect your subscribers:

- Never add people without permission
- Provide consistent value in every message
- Maintain regular but not excessive contact
- Make unsubscribing simple and painless
- Honor privacy regulations (GDPR, CAN-SPAM, etc.)

Breaking these rules doesn't just risk legal trouble—it destroys trust.

DO NOT SPAM READERS WITH BOOK LINKS

The Difference Between Spam and Smart Marketing

Bad: "Buy my book now! Link in bio!"

Good: "Struggling with publishing mistakes? Here's the checklist I wish I had when I started."

Bad: Dropping links in every Facebook group without context.

Good: Sharing insights from your publishing journey that naturally lead readers to your book.

Bad: "Hey new follower, check out my book!"

Good: Building real relationships that make people curious about your work.

The best-selling authors rarely "sell" directly. They share generously, build communities, and create such strong value that readers want to support them naturally.

Aggressive promotion pushes readers away. Authentic connection pulls them closer.

You can't just throw a link at the internet and hope for the best. If you want readers to care about your book, give them a reason to care about you first.

Smart marketing isn't louder marketing—it's better connection. Build that, and your books will sell themselves.

DO NOT RELY ON OCCASIONAL SOCIAL POSTS

Many authors assume that social media is an easy path to book sales. They spend hours posting on Instagram, tweeting about their book, and sharing their Amazon link in Facebook groups—only to realize they're making little to no sales.

Social media **can** drive book sales, but only when used strategically as part of a complete marketing approach. Random posting and hoping for results isn't a strategy—it's wishful thinking.

The Social Media Reality Check

Social media fails authors when they:

- Focus on follower count rather than follower engagement
- Post the same content across all platforms regardless of fit

- Share only promotional content without building relationships
- Expect immediate sales from casual posting
- Neglect to create clear paths from social platforms to sales
- Misunderstand platform algorithms and audience behaviors

Why casual posting doesn't sell books:

- Algorithms prioritize engagement, not promotional content
- Followers need multiple touchpoints before purchasing
- Book buying is emotional, requiring deeper connection
- Passive scrolling rarely converts to active buying
- Social platforms are designed for social interaction, not direct sales

The TikTok Effect — How BookTok Transformed Book Marketing

TikTok has created a phenomenon unlike any other platform through its BookTok community. Authors who understand it have seen explosive success:

- Readers showing genuine emotional reactions to books
- Viral content driving thousands of sales overnight

- Publishers creating specific BookTok tables in stores
- Backlist titles suddenly becoming bestsellers years after release
- New authors finding massive audiences through reader advocacy

Why BookTok works when random posting doesn't:

- Authenticity drives the platform (genuine reader reactions)
- Emotional responses are prioritized over polished content
- Community discussion matters more than author promotion
- Algorithm supports niche content reaching relevant audiences
- Video format creates stronger emotional connections

Successful BookTok strategies:

- Share behind-the-scenes of your writing process
- Create aesthetic content that matches your book's vibe
- Highlight emotional moments without spoilers
- Participate in book-related trends and challenges
- Engage directly with readers through comments and duets

Effective Social Media Strategies That Actually Sell Books

1. Build a Community, Not Just a Following

Focus on genuine connections:

- Respond to every comment when possible
- Ask questions that invite conversation
- Create content that encourages sharing and discussion
- Highlight reader experiences with your books
- Share personal (but professional) glimpses into your author life
- Make followers feel like valued community members

People don't just buy books—they invest in authors they feel connected to.

2. Create Platform-Specific Content

Each social platform has unique strengths:

- Instagram: Visual aesthetics, lifestyle content, Stories
- TikTok: Authentic, emotion-driven short videos
- Twitter: Industry connections, conversations, quick updates
- Facebook: Groups, longer content, community building
- Pinterest: Discoverability, mood boards, visual inspiration
- LinkedIn: Professional connections, thought leadership (nonfiction)

Don't simply copy/paste across platforms. Tailor content to fit each space.

3. Use the 80/20 Rule

Effective social media follows the 80/20 rule:

- 80% value-driven, engaging, non-promotional content
- 20% direct promotion and sales messaging
- Focus on entertainment, education, and inspiration
- Build trust before asking for the sale
- Demonstrate your value before promoting your books

This keeps followers engaged and prevents them from tuning out.

4. Convert Followers Into Email Subscribers

Social media is "rented land." Email lists are "owned land."

- Offer valuable lead magnets related to your books
- Create platform-specific landing pages for each social channel
- Track conversion rates from social media to email
- Develop a welcome sequence for social media subscribers
- Use email to nurture relationships built through social platforms

Building your list creates a direct line to your most interested readers.

5. Collaborate With Other Authors and Influencers

Cross-promotion amplifies your exposure:

- Partner with authors in complementary genres
- Arrange takeovers of each other's accounts
- Participate in multi-author challenges or events
- Engage authentically with book influencers
- Create joint content that serves both audiences

Collaboration multiplies your marketing reach without doubling your effort.

6. Implement Social-Specific Sales Funnels

Treat social media like a smart sales funnel:

- Create platform-specific links to track where sales originate
- Develop unique landing pages for social media traffic
- Monitor which content types drive actual conversions
- Adjust strategy based on results, not assumptions
- Implement retargeting for social media visitors to your website

Marketing without measurement is just noise.

Beyond Social Media: Build a Complete Marketing Plan

Social media should be part of a multi-channel strategy:

- Author website with email capture

- Strategic Amazon presence (categories, keywords, reviews)
- Paid advertising when appropriate
- Media and podcast appearances
- Direct reader outreach
- Retailer and bookstore relationships
- Content marketing beyond social platforms

Social media alone isn't enough. A holistic strategy builds lasting success.

Social Media Success Requires Strategy, Not Hype

To make social media work for book sales, you must be:

- Consistent in your presence
- Strategic in your content
- Authentic in your engagement
- Focused on building relationships
- Patient with the conversion process
- Adaptable as platforms evolve

Random posting won't sell your book. Strategic engagement will.

Social media isn't a magic solution—but when used wisely, it becomes a powerful engine for discovery, connection, and sales. Approach it like a professional, not a casual user, and you'll see the difference.

DO NOT AVOID PAID ADVERTISING

Many self-published authors avoid advertising like it's a communicable disease. They convince themselves it's too expensive, too complicated, or flat-out doesn't work. Others throw money at random platforms without a plan, then act shocked when sales don't materialize.

Both approaches miss what's actually happening: strategic advertising has become essential in today's publishing landscape. Period.

Book Discovery Has Fundamentally Changed

Let's face it—readers don't find books like they used to:

- Physical bookstores have dramatically decreased in number
- Online algorithms prioritize already-successful titles
- Millions of new books compete for limited attention

- Social media organic reach continues to decline
- Newsletter and email open rates are dropping
- Browser searches prioritize paid results

In this reality, well-targeted paid advertising gives you something priceless: access to readers actively searching for books like yours. This isn't an expense—it's an investment in visibility that free methods simply can't deliver anymore.

Where Your Advertising Dollars Actually Work

Not all platforms are created equal. Focus on these:

Amazon Ads

Amazon works because you're reaching people already shopping for books. Your ad appears right when someone is ready to buy.

Use Amazon ads for:

- Targeting specific author and genre searches
- Promoting backlist titles alongside your newest release
- Capturing sales during high-conversion moments
- Building visibility within competitive categories
- Driving immediate sales with direct ROI tracking

The beauty? The reader is already in "buying mode"—they're browsing with a credit card ready.

BookBub Ads

BookBub lets you target readers by specific author interests. You're reaching dedicated book lovers who've signed up specifically to discover new titles.

Use BookBub ads for:

- Targeting fans of comparable authors
- Promoting limited-time price promotions
- Building visibility for series starters
- Reaching dedicated genre readers
- Supporting BookBub Featured Deal campaigns

Facebook/Instagram Ads

These platforms require smarter targeting but excel at reaching readers who match your audience profile—even when they're not actively book shopping.

Use Facebook and Instagram ads for:

- Building your email subscriber list
- Creating awareness for new releases
- Promoting reader magnets and lead generation
- Retargeting website visitors who didn't purchase
- Reaching demographically similar audiences to your readers

Why Your Ads Are Failing

When authors say "advertising doesn't work," they've usually made these mistakes:

- Running generic ads to untargeted audiences
- Failing to track results beyond the immediate sale
- Using weak or unprofessional creative assets
- Setting unrealistic expectations for early campaigns
- Giving up before collecting sufficient data
- Not testing different approaches systematically
- Ignoring the lifetime value of acquired readers

The biggest mistake? Expecting immediate profits from your first campaigns. Smart advertisers understand that early campaigns are primarily data collection—profitability comes after refining everything based on real results.

How to Start Advertising Without Losing Your Mind (or Savings)

If you've been avoiding advertising, here's your roadmap:

Step 1: Get Clear on Your Goals

Define exactly what success looks like:

- New release visibility
- Series starter promotion
- Email list building
- Backlist revival
- Author brand awareness

Different goals demand different ad approaches.

Step 2: Start With a Learning Budget

Begin with a modest budget—$5–$10 per day for 30 days on one platform. This isn't about immediate profit. It's about buying yourself an education. The insights you gain will be worth far more than the money spent.

Step 3: Master One Platform First

Don't spread yourself thin. For most authors, Amazon Ads provide the clearest, most direct path to understanding buyer behavior.

Step 4: Track Everything

Even a simple spreadsheet tracking:

- Ad spend per day
- Impressions and clicks
- Sales and page reads
- Cost per click (CPC)
- Advertising cost of sales (ACoS)

...will show you patterns quickly. Get fancy later—start simple now.

Step 5: Test Systematically

Test only one variable at a time:

- Different ad copy
- Various audience targets
- Alternative images
- Price points
- Landing pages

Controlled testing tells you exactly what works—and what doesn't.

How to Make Advertising Actually Profitable

Think Beyond the Single Sale

The goal isn't just covering ad spend on one book. It's acquiring readers who buy across your entire catalog.

Example: If a reader spends $30 across your series, you're thrilled to spend $10 to acquire them.

This changes everything about how you view ad spending.

Build Funnels, Not Just Ads

Smart author marketers create multi-stage systems:

- Low-priced or free entry points
- Email capture for long-term relationship building
- Upsells to higher-priced products
- Backend offers for loyal readers
- Referral and word-of-mouth incentives

Advertising feeds your larger author business—not just single book sales.

Time Your Ad Spending Strategically

Match ads with:

- New releases
- Price promotions

- Seasonal themes
- Category trends
- Real-world events
- Media mentions

Momentum matters.

Scale What Works (Carefully)

When you find a winning ad:

- Increase budget by 20% at a time
- Expand to similar audiences
- Create variations of successful creatives
- Test on complementary platforms
- Invest in more sophisticated tracking

Scaling too fast burns out audiences and kills otherwise profitable ads.

Successful author advertisers treat ads like a long-term investment—allocating steady budgets, constantly testing, and evolving based on real results.

Advertising Isn't Optional Anymore

In today's publishing landscape, avoiding paid advertising means voluntarily restricting your visibility.

You don't need massive budgets or a marketing degree. You need:

- Willingness to learn systematically

- Patience with the testing process
- Commitment to data-based decisions
- Understanding of reader psychology
- Clear goals beyond immediate ROI

The real question isn't, "Can I afford to advertise?" It's, "Can I afford for no one to know my book exists?"

Start smart. Build gradually. Your future readers are out there—you just have to reach them.

DO NOT IGNORE DISCOVERABILITY: METADATA, KEYWORDS, AND ALTERNATIVE SALES CHANNELS

I initially dismissed metadata as unnecessary because it went over my head. But when I realized it's the critical barrier between visibility and obscurity for my book in the digital marketplace, everything changed. Similarly, I watched countless sales vanish because I relied solely on Amazon instead of exploring the full range of places readers actually shop.

You can write the most life-changing book in existence, but without proper metadata, keywords, and distribution across multiple sales channels, you might as well have kept it in your desk drawer. The harsh reality? Your perfect reader could be desperately searching for exactly what you've created, but if they can't find it, you'll never meet.

What Is Metadata and Why Does It Matter?

Metadata is all the background information attached to your book that helps retailers, libraries, and search engines categorize, display, and recommend it. This includes:

- Title and subtitle
- Author name and bio
- Book description
- Categories/BISAC codes
- Keywords
- ISBN
- Publisher information
- Page count and format details

If your metadata isn't optimized, your book will struggle to appear in search results—no matter how good it is.

Keywords: The Search Engine Connection

Keywords directly influence whether your book appears in searches. Readers rarely type a book title unless they already know about it. Instead, they search for phrases like:

- "Romance novels with strong female characters"
- "Self-help books for procrastination"
- "Fantasy with unique magic systems"
- "How to start an online business"

If your book isn't connected to these searches through strong keywords, it simply won't appear.

How Amazon's Algorithm Works

Amazon acts like a search engine. Keywords influence:

- Which readers see your book in search results
- Which "also bought" lists include your title
- What recommendations Amazon sends via email
- Whether your book appears in advertisements

Optimizing Your Metadata Elements

Title & Subtitle — Clear and Searchable

Good Examples:

- "Marketing Made Simple: A Step-by-Step Guide for Small Business Owners"
- "The Night Hunters: A Supernatural Thriller"

Bad Examples:
- "Dreams" (too vague, no keywords)
- "The Journey of a Thousand Stars Throughout the Cosmos of Love and Life" (too flowery, unclear genre)

Pro Tip: Use your subtitle to naturally add important keywords.

Book Description — More Than Just a Summary

An optimized book description should:

- Begin with a hook that captures attention
- Include relevant keywords naturally throughout
- Maintain readable, compelling language
- End with a clear call to action

Beyond One Storefront: Reaching Readers Everywhere

Many authors make a costly mistake: they release their book on one major marketplace, then stop. They treat it as the final step instead of the beginning of a real distribution strategy.

Relying on a single platform—no matter how large—severely limits your reach. Readers exist across a broad landscape of marketplaces, communities, and specialized platforms that often serve their needs better.

The Power of Specialized Marketplaces

Niche marketplaces focus on serving specific audiences with precision and intentionality:

• Genre-specific retailers like Smashwords or Draft2Digital connect you with dedicated readers

• Specialty bookstores like Kobo for international audiences or Book Funnel for direct sales target distinct communities

• Subscription services like Scribd or Kindle Unlimited provide recurring revenue streams

• Niche platforms like Radish for serialized fiction or Wattpad for younger readers offer unique discovery opportunities

The readers in these communities are pre-qualified: they are actively looking for exactly the kind of work you have created. Visibility is stronger, competition is often lower, and trust is built more easily through aligned values.

Expanding Internationally

Significant reading populations exist beyond primary English-speaking markets:

• International Amazon stores open your book to readers globally, each with different browsing patterns and preferences

• Kobo's strong presence in Canada, Australia, and New Zealand creates new reader communities

• Apple Books and Google Play maintain dedicated international storefronts with local payment systems

• Developing market platforms like BooksaMillion or 24Symbols reach readers in regions with rapidly growing digital adoption

International distribution is not optional for authors serious about career growth—it is essential.

Integrating Keywords and Distribution For Maximum Discovery

The most successful authors combine powerful metadata with strategic distribution:

1. Research keywords using Amazon's search suggestion, competitive analysis, and reader language
2. Optimize metadata across all platforms, adjusting for each marketplace's unique algorithm
3. Distribute strategically to multiple channels, including niche marketplaces aligned with your genre
4. Track performance across platforms to identify where your book resonates most strongly

5. Adjust based on data, refining keywords and prioritizing high-converting channels

Implementation Checklist

- Set aside dedicated time for keyword research
- Create platform-specific metadata files for each major retailer
- Develop a distribution plan that includes at least 3-5 sales channels
- Establish tracking systems to monitor performance
- Schedule quarterly metadata reviews to keep your book discoverable

Your book deserves to be discovered by the right readers—readers who need exactly what you've created. Don't let poor metadata or limited distribution hide your work from the very people searching for it. The difference between obscurity and visibility isn't just quality—it's discoverability through strategic metadata and comprehensive distribution.

DO NOT ABANDON YOUR AUTHOR WEBSITE

I own a website. I've had it for years now. I didn't outsource the design either—I built it myself (and have designed others). Yet, for a long time, it just collected dust while I exhausted myself chasing likes, comments, and followers on Facebook and Instagram.

Why? Because the dopamine rush of real-time notifications feels good. But reality hit hard: I had my priorities completely backward. While obsessing over social validation, I neglected building the only platform I truly control.

Your website isn't just another marketing checkbox—it's your digital property. You own it.

Social media platforms are rented spaces. The landlord (the platform) can—and will—change the locks without warning. Your website? It's your deeded land. It's yours no matter what new algorithm, trend, or policy comes next.

When retailer policies shift and author pages disappear, or when your social media reach plummets overnight, your website remains your constant—your professional home base where readers can always find you.

The Non-Negotiable Website Elements

If you're serious about your author career, your website must include:

Professional Design

Align it with your genre. Romance readers expect softness; thriller readers expect edge. Your website should visually match your book covers and brand identity. First impressions form in seconds—make yours count.

A Compelling Author Bio

Skip the credential list. Tell the story behind why you write what you write. Let readers see the human behind the books—they connect with people, not resumes.

Individual Book Pages with Purchase Options

Create a page for each book with direct links to every place readers can buy it. Never make readers hunt for your work. Make buying easy.

Newsletter Signup Everywhere

Your email list is your most powerful marketing tool. Offer something meaningful—a free chapter, bonus content, a special story—in exchange for their email address.

Professional Contact Method

Make it easy for media, event organizers, or readers to reach you. Create accessibility without compromising your privacy.

Beyond the Basics: Building a Stronger Digital Home

Want to go further? Add:

• **Blog or Content Hub**: Regular updates give readers reasons to return and improve your search visibility

• **Media Kit**: Make it easy for journalists, podcasters, and reviewers to feature you

• **Event Calendar**: Show where you'll be appearing, whether virtually or in person

• **Reader Resources**: Character guides, series timelines, or bonus materials that enhance the reading experience

• **Testimonials and Reviews**: Social proof builds credibility with new visitors

• **FAQ Section**: Answer common questions to save time and establish expectations

Why Your Website Matters More Than You Think

Your website does what social media never will:

• Gives you complete control over messaging and branding

• Creates a professional impression with media and industry professionals

- Serves as your searchable hub when readers look for you online

- Provides direct conversion paths to email signups and book sales

- Archives your entire catalog, regardless of retailer availability

- Builds long-term SEO value that compounds over time

- Offers analytics you own and can truly understand

Let's Kill Those Weak Excuses

"I don't know how." → Website builders today are as easy to use as posting on Facebook. No coding needed.

"It's too expensive." → Domains cost about $15/year. Hosting is $10/month. That's cheaper than your coffee habit.

"I don't have time." → Update your website quarterly. Two hours every three months. No excuses.

"Social media is better." → Social media and websites are not competitors—they serve different purposes. Social creates attention. Your website creates permanence.

Your website is your digital headquarters.

It's the one place where you control the rules, the experience, and the future of your author business. Every book you publish makes your website more valuable. Every reader you reach strengthens it.

Treat your website with the same care you give your writing:

Build it with intention
Make it professional
Make it reader-friendly
Keep it alive

This is your house on the internet. Own it. Protect it. Grow it. Because nothing else—no retailer, no social platform—can guarantee you lasting access to your audience. Your website can.

DO NOT NEGLECT TO BUILD A READER COMMUNITY

Publishing a book isn't your finish line—it's the starting point of a relationship with your readers.

I've watched too many authors chase the high of launch day, only to crash when sales inevitably slow. The authors who build sustainable careers aren't constantly hustling for new readers with each release. They build communities of engaged fans who return, book after book, year after year.

Beyond Transactions: Creating True Fans

Stop obsessing over one-time transactions. That "units sold" metric you're fixated on? It's the wrong focus.

There's a profound difference between someone who buys your book once and a true fan who connects with your work on a deeper level.

True fans pre-order your next book without seeing a cover. They leave thoughtful reviews without you begging. They recommend your work to friends. They show up to your events and respond to your emails.

Relationships—not fleeting transactions—sustain author careers through algorithm changes, market shifts, and industry upheaval.

Email: Your Most Powerful Relationship Tool

I don't care how many Instagram followers you have. Social media platforms own those followers—not you.

Email puts you in control. When readers subscribe to your list, they invite you directly into their inbox—a personal space no algorithm can block.

The data is clear:

- Email subscribers are 5-10 times more likely to buy your book than social followers
- Email open rates typically range from 20-40%, while social reach often falls below 5%
- Email subscribers spend more on average than one-time buyers
- Direct email communication builds deeper, more personal connections
- You own your list regardless of which platforms come and go

Email subscribers buy books at dramatically higher rates than social followers.

Building Your Email Foundation

Start building your email list immediately:

- Create a compelling lead magnet: free short story, character guide, or valuable resource
- Place signup forms prominently on your website
- Offer exclusive content not available elsewhere
- Maintain consistent, value-driven communication
- Segment your list to deliver targeted content
- Track essential metrics (opens, clicks, conversions)

What you put in these emails matters. Balance promotion with value—share writing insights, behind-the-scenes stories, and personal updates. Follow the 80/20 principle: 80% valuable content, 20% direct promotion.

Creating Community Spaces

Expand beyond email by creating dedicated spaces where readers can connect with each other:

- Private Facebook or Discord groups for deeper discussions
- Book club questions and virtual meetups
- Reader forums on your website
- Virtual events like Q&A sessions or character interviews
- In-person meetups at conferences or local venues

- Shared creative spaces for fan art, fan fiction, or discussions

Effective reader communities offer value beyond promotional updates. They give readers opportunities to:

- Connect with like-minded people who share their interests
- Access exclusive content and experiences
- Participate in the creative process through feedback
- Develop personal connections with you and your work
- Feel recognized and valued for their support
- Contribute to something meaningful

The Rhythm of Sustainable Relationships

Don't only appear when you have something to sell. The relationships built during the "off-season" between launches often prove the most valuable.

Genre matters when planning your approach. Fiction readers thrive on character discussions and world-building. Nonfiction readers focus on transformation, expertise, and learning.

Launch Power and Long-Term Payoffs

When launch day comes, an established reader community becomes your greatest asset.

They provide concentrated day-one sales that boost your visibility and ranking. They deliver early reviews that fuel word-of-mouth promotion. They create organic momentum that is impossible to buy.

Building a community also opens doors beyond book sales:

- Speaking opportunities through word-of-mouth
- Collaboration invitations from other authors
- Media attention from consistent visibility
- Merchandising and auxiliary product opportunities
- Direct support through crowdfunding or patronage
- Personal satisfaction from meaningful reader connections

Managing Community Sustainably

Set clear boundaries. You are an author first—not a 24/7 community manager.

Stay legally compliant. When collecting emails, always follow GDPR, CAN-SPAM, and CASL regulations. Reputable email services help maintain compliance, but know the basics yourself.

Your Most Valuable Asset

Building a reader community isn't about selling one book—it's about creating relationships that sustain your career.

Your current book isn't your most valuable asset. The community of readers who will follow you through every future project is.

Your reader community creates stability when everything else shifts. Social media platforms rise and fall. Algorithms change without warning. Retail policies can wipe out entire marketing strategies overnight.

Through all these changes, your direct connection to readers remains your foundation.

Stop wasting thousands of hours chasing followers and likes. Start building real relationships that turn readers into loyal supporters.

Your next success won't come from platform hacks or lucky algorithms. It will come from the community you intentionally build—starting now.

DO NOT WAIT FOR MEDIA TO DISCOVER YOUR BOOK

Countless authors publish their books, sit back, and wait for *The New York Times* to call. Spoiler alert: it's not happening. Your book is just one among thousands released today. Traditional media won't take notice—until you make them notice.

Why Traditional Media Still Matters

Social media and online ads help, but ignoring traditional media cuts you off from powerful exposure that most authors never tap into. Media coverage gives you:

- Credibility that self-promotion cannot match
- Access to audiences who might never find you online
- Valuable content to share across your platforms
- Third-party validation that builds trust
- Evergreen material for your press kit and website
- Momentum that can lead to more media opportunities

One author I worked with landed a 10-minute slot on a small local morning show discussing her book about urban gardening. That single interview led to three speaking engagements, a newspaper feature, and steady book sales for months. All from one well-executed media pitch.

The Three Deadly Media Pitch Mistakes

First mistake: Waiting to be discovered. Journalists aren't trolling Amazon looking for new releases. They're overworked and overwhelmed. If you're not pitching them directly, you don't exist to them.

Second mistake: Writing a press release that reads like an ad. Journalists want a *story*, not a sales pitch. Compare:

- "Award-winning novel now available on Amazon!" (boring)
- "Local teacher's debut novel explores opioid crisis affecting rural communities" (newsworthy)

One screams "Buy my book." The other offers a real cultural hook.

Third mistake: Mass-blasting the same boring pitch to everyone. татьTV needs visuals. Radio needs personality. Magazines want depth and angles. If you don't tailor your pitch for each outlet, it shows—and it gets deleted.

I worked with an author who pitched her cookbook three ways: to TV stations focusing on colorful dishes, to radio hosts discussing family traditions, and to magazines covering seasonal foods. She secured coverage across all three by respecting each platform's needs.

How to Create a Press Release That Actually Works

Your press release should give journalists everything they need to turn your announcement into a compelling story.

Start with a headline that stops them in their tracks:

- "Former Hostage Negotiator Reveals Communication Tactics in New Book"
- "Local Author's Research Uncovers Forgotten Civil Rights Hero"
- "New Thriller Predicted Current Political Crisis Six Months Ago"

First paragraph: Get straight to the point. In two or three sentences, answer: Who? What? When? Where? Why does it matter?

Example: *"Award-winning psychologist Dr. Regina Mayfield releases Rewired, a groundbreaking guide to anxiety management during America's mental health crisis. Based on ten years of clinical research, the book challenges conventional treatments and offers new hope. Mayfield will speak at Hartford Memorial Hospital on June 15."*

Second paragraph: Zoom in on your unique angle. Tie your book to something bigger happening right now. Connect it to real-world trends, news, or community concerns.

Third paragraph: Establish your authority. Why should a journalist trust you? Mention real credentials, experiences, or achievements—not just vague claims.

Finally, make it ridiculously easy to contact you. Include your name, email, phone, and a direct link to a professional press kit (with high-res images, sample interview questions, book excerpt, and anything else they'd need).

Where to Send It

Spraying your press release everywhere won't help. Target smart:

- Local media first—they're most likely to cover you
- Industry publications related to your topic
- Podcast hosts and YouTube channels in your niche
- Journalists who've covered similar books or authors
- Regional shows and publications that align with your book's themes
- National outlets with specific sections matching your topic

Follow up once about a week later. Be polite. Offer something specific, like a free review copy or an exclusive quote.

Most pitches get ignored. That's normal. Your job isn't to beg for attention—it's to present your book as part of a bigger story people already care about. When you show up as a resource, not a salesperson, you start getting yeses instead of silence.

The authors who land interviews, features, and articles aren't always the most talented writers—they're the ones who understand how media works and meet journalists halfway.

You don't wait for permission to be discovered. You *create* the opportunity.

DO NOT BUY FAKE REVIEWS

That empty review section on your new Amazon book listing is a special kind of torture. Zero feedback. Zero validation. I've watched authors stare at their screens for days, refreshing the page, desperate for someone—anyone—to leave a comment. When nothing comes, the temptation arrives: websites promising "guaranteed 5-star reviews" for just a few dollars.

Don't do it. I'm dead serious.

Purchasing fake reviews isn't a marketing strategy—it's career suicide wrapped in a momentary dopamine hit.

Amazon's detection systems are sophisticated and constantly improving. They track language patterns, posting behavior, IP addresses, and suspicious reviewer-author connections. When (not if) these systems flag your book, the punishment is swift and merciless:

The legal risks are real, too. The Federal Trade Commission classifies undisclosed paid reviews as deceptive advertising—a violation that can lead to hefty fines and legal action. No amount of temporary visibility is worth risking your entire financial future.

And even if you somehow slipped past detection? Fake reviews still sabotage your real career.

When genuine readers buy your book based on inflated praise, the reality often disappoints. That gap between expectation and experience triggers harsh reviews—the kind that burn trust, kill word-of-mouth momentum, and permanently damage your reputation.

Literary communities are intimate. News spreads fast. If you're caught buying fake reviews, good luck finding real supporters among readers, bloggers, book clubs, or other authors. The stain on your name won't wash off easily.

How to Build Real Reviews Instead

Skip the shortcuts and focus on what actually works:

Every bestselling author once had zero reviews. Everyone. Review growth happens organically as readers find your work, connect with it, and feel moved to comment. It takes time. But it creates a real foundation for long-term success.

Five thoughtful, honest reviews from real readers will always outperform fifty generic, purchased comments. Real reviews highlight what truly resonates—and that pulls your next reader closer.

Building your review base takes patience. It takes persistence. It requires protecting your brand even when it feels painfully slow. But it's the only path that builds an actual, lasting career.

Your work deserves real appreciation. Your reputation deserves real protection. Don't sacrifice it for a hollow illusion of success.

DO NOT ARGUE WITH REVIEWERS

Bad reviews happen to every author—period. Doesn't matter how good your book is. Bestselling authors with massive followings get eviscerated by one-star reviews. Why? Because books are subjective. Some readers won't connect with your writing, and they'll make sure everyone knows it.

Here's what you need to internalize right now: A bad review is not a personal attack. It's someone's opinion about your work—not a verdict on your worth as a writer or human being. If you let negative feedback destroy your confidence, you'll never grow. Learning to handle criticism without breaking down is essential to your longevity as an author.

Why Bad Reviews Happen (And Why They're Actually Valuable)

No Book Pleases Everyone

Look at literary history. Some readers call To Kill a Mockingbird boring. Others dismiss Harry Potter as overhyped. Some find The Great Gatsby pointless. When your book gets a few harsh reviews, it simply means you've expanded your reach beyond your core audience. That's actually progress.

Readers Bring Their Own Expectations

Every person who opens your book carries different preferences and biases. Some crave fast-paced action while others want character-driven reflections. Some seek profound messages while others just want entertainment. When expectations don't align with what you've written, negative reviews follow—even if your execution was flawless for what you intended to create.

Negative Reviews Build Credibility

A book with only five-star ratings raises immediate suspicion. Readers wonder if only friends and family provided feedback. A healthy mix of opinions shows real engagement.

Sometimes the very thing a critical reviewer hates becomes your selling point. When someone writes, "Too much detailed world-building," they're actually attracting readers who love immersive settings.

How to Handle Criticism Without Losing Your Mind

Never Engage With Reviewers

This is non-negotiable: Do not respond to negative reviews. Ever. Arguing with readers makes you look insecure and unprofessional. One defensive comment can transform a single bad review into a public relations nightmare.

Readers have the right to their opinions, however misguided they might seem. If you can't resist the temptation to respond, stop reading your reviews altogether.

Extract the Valuable Feedback

Some negative reviews contain genuine insights that can improve your craft. When multiple reviewers point out slow pacing, consider tightening your next book. If grammar complaints surface repeatedly, invest in better editing before your next release. If people consistently misunderstand your premise, revisit your marketing materials.

A thoughtful three-star review often teaches more valuable lessons than a vague five-star rating.

Maintain Perspective

One harsh critique feels devastating in the moment but represents a single voice among many. Readers rarely make purchase decisions based on isolated reviews—they consider overall ratings and patterns.

Every successful book on the market has its share of one-star reviews. When you've accumulated fifty-plus reviews with a 4.2-star average, you're succeeding. A handful of dissenters can't change that reality.

Keep Creating

The most resilient response to criticism is continued productivity. If Stephen King had surrendered after early criticism of Carrie, we'd have lost dozens of cultural touchstones. If J.K. Rowling had crumbled under rejection, Harry Potter would never have transformed children's literature.

The most powerful answer to a negative review is your next book.

Reviews Are for Readers, Not Authors

Bad reviews come with the territory. Every published book attracts them, and they don't define your story's value. Don't let strangers' opinions derail your creative purpose.

Reaching a wide audience guarantees some readers won't connect with your work—that's not failure, it's mathematics. Your responsibility is to write, improve, and persist.

Not every book resonates with every reader, but every authentic book finds its people. The only definitive failure in writing is quitting.

DO NOT USE MISLEADING ADVERTISING

Marketing your book is non-negotiable, but how you promote it will determine whether you build a career or destroy it before it begins.

Many authors sabotage themselves with exaggerated claims—calling their books "bestsellers" after hitting #1 in an obscure Amazon subcategory for two hours, comparing themselves to Eric Jerome Dickey when they write nothing like him, or touting "awards" from competitions nobody's ever heard of.

These aren't just harmless marketing tactics. They're ticking time bombs.

When readers feel misled, they don't just leave bad reviews—they demand refunds, report you to retailers, and never buy your work again. Amazon has a zero-tolerance policy for deceptive practices, and they'll suspend your account with little warning.

Deceptive Marketing: The Road to Career Suicide

Many authors blur the line between smart promotion and outright deception without realizing it. Here's what to avoid:

Fake Bestseller Claims: Hitting #1 in "Historical Fantasy Romance for Left-Handed Readers" isn't the same as being a "bestselling author." Period.

False Author Comparisons: Unless your mystery genuinely resembles Walter Mosley s style, don't promise readers "perfect for Mosley fans." You're setting up disappointment.

Fabricated Recognition: That $50 "award" from a website nobody's heard of? Readers can smell that scam from miles away.

Undisclosed Paid Reviews: Paying for reviews violates Amazon's terms and FTC guidelines. And yes, they can tell when you're doing it.

Misleading Packaging: If your cover and blurb promise an epic fantasy but deliver a romance with minor magical elements, prepare for backlash.

Artificial Scarcity: Claiming "only 100 copies available" for a digital product is both ridiculous and unethical.

Every time you exaggerate or mislead, you're gambling with your entire publishing future.

The Very Real Legal Consequences

This isn't just about ethics—it's about law. The publishing industry is regulated by:

DO NOT USE MISLEADING ADVERTISING

FTC Regulations: The Federal Trade Commission rigorously enforces advertising laws, particularly for digital products.

Platform-Specific Rules: Amazon, Facebook, and other platforms have strict guidelines about promotional claims.

International Standards: The UK's Advertising Standards Authority and EU consumer protection laws apply to your global marketing.

Violate these, and you face:

- Account suspension or permanent bans
- Lawsuits from misled consumers
- Removal from distribution channels
- Fines and legal penalties
- Permanent reputation damage

Honest Marketing That Actually Works

You don't need to lie to sell books. Here's what works better:

Bestseller Claims That Hold Water

Only use "bestseller" when you can prove it:

- New York Times Bestseller List
- USA Today Bestseller List
- Wall Street Journal Bestseller List
- Publisher's Weekly Bestseller List
- National newspaper bestseller lists

Instead of vague "bestselling author" claims, try specifics: "Reached #7 in Amazon Historical Fiction" (if true).

Transparent About Recognition

If your book won an award, name it specifically: "Winner of the 2023 Independent Book Awards - Romance Category."

Vague "award-winning" claims without details scream amateur and erode trust.

For reviews, always disclose connections. An honest "my writing group loved this book" is better than pretending those reviews came from strangers.

Author Comparisons That Make Sense

Instead of claiming "for fans of Colleen Hoover" when your writing bears no resemblance to hers, try: "For readers who enjoy emotional family dramas with complex female protagonists."

When you do make comparisons, be specific about the connection: "Features fast-paced legal thrillers in the tradition of John Grisham and Scott Turow."

Honest Pricing Strategies

Never claim:

- "Limited time only" for permanent pricing
- "75% off" when the book was never sold at full price
- "Retail value $29.99" for a book that never sold at that price

Instead, focus on genuine value: "Special launch price" or "Anniversary discount."

Authentic Review Building

Forbidden tactics:

- Paying for reviews (directly or through "book review services")
- Review swapping ("I'll 5-star yours if you 5-star mine")
- Family/friend reviews without disclosure
- Review manipulation ("only leave a review if you loved it")

Better approaches:

- Sending advance reader copies (ARCs) to genuine readers
- Including a simple "If you enjoyed this book, please consider leaving a review" at the back
- Building an authentic reader community who supports your work honestly

Ethical Marketing That Drives Real Sales

The most powerful marketing tool is authenticity. Try these proven approaches:

- Tell your genuine author story: Why you wrote this book, what inspired it, who it's truly for

- Share your expertise: What qualifies you to write this story or teach this subject
- Build real reader relationships: Engage authentically with your audience
- Showcase legitimate editorial reviews: From credible sources who've actually read your work
- Create value first: Offer free content that demonstrates your writing quality
- Be transparent about your book: What it is, what it isn't, who will love it, who might not

False marketing creates one-time buyers. Honest marketing creates lifetime readers.

Respect your audience enough to be authentic. They'll reward you with the only thing that matters in this business: genuine loyalty.

DO NOT UNDERESTIMATE BOOK TRAILERS

If you're ignoring video marketing for your book, you're missing valuable opportunities. Today's readers are scrolling through TikTok, Instagram, and YouTube—and if you're not there with a compelling book trailer, you're invisible.

Many authors resist this reality, believing book trailers are only for major publishers or beyond their budget. This mindset costs them sales and visibility daily.

The statistics are compelling: videos on social media generate 1200% more shares than text and images combined. Viewers retain 95% of a message when watching video, compared to just 10% when reading text. These numbers represent the difference between a book that sells and one that collects digital dust.

Creating Effective Book Trailers Without Breaking the Bank

You don't need expensive equipment or specialized training. A smartphone and basic editing apps can create effective content. Platforms like Canva and Adobe Express offer templates specifically designed for book trailers that look professional with minimal effort.

Effective book trailers trigger emotional connections in 60-90 seconds. For novels, focus on mood and conflict. For self-help books, demonstrate the transformation readers will experience. Rather than explaining what your book is about, show why readers need it.

Maximizing Your Trailer's Impact Through Strategic Distribution

Distribution is as important as creation. Instagram Reels, TikTok, and Facebook prioritize video content in their algorithms. You can repurpose the same trailer across different platforms to reach diverse audiences. Amazon's Author Central accepts video uploads, creating another touchpoint where buyers make decisions.

Your book trailer isn't just marketing—it's a versatile asset. Include it in your media kit when approaching podcasts or blogs. Embed it in email newsletters to boost click-through rates. Share it with book clubs considering your title. Each use extends your reach without additional work.

The Hidden Benefits of Creating a Book Trailer

Creating a trailer clarifies your entire marketing message. Distilling your book into 60 seconds of visuals helps identify what truly matters. This clarity improves everything from your elevator pitch to your Amazon description.

For budget-conscious authors, stock footage sites like Pexels and Pixabay offer free high-quality video clips. Royalty-free music sites provide atmospheric soundtracks for minimal investment. If you need help, Fiverr connects you with video editors at surprisingly affordable rates.

Authenticity often outperforms production quality. A sincere video where you simply talk about why you wrote your book can create stronger connections than an expensive production. Readers respond to genuine passion.

Elements of Effective Book Trailers

The most effective book trailers consistently:

- Open with a hook that creates immediate curiosity
- Establish a clear emotional tone matching the book
- Use compelling visuals that support the core premise
- Include professional-looking title and author cards
- End with a clear call to action ("Available now on...")
- Keep pacing tight with no unnecessary content
- Maintain high audio quality (poor sound ruins trailers faster than anything)

The publishing landscape grows more crowded every day. In this environment, book trailers aren't luxury items—they're essential tools for visibility. As video continues dominating digital communication, refusing to adapt means accepting irrelevance.

TAKE SELF OUT OF SELF PUBLISHING

Your book represents countless hours of work and tremendous personal investment. Don't let it disappear into the void because you weren't willing to create a trailer. In today's visual world, helping readers see your book is the first step toward getting them to read it.

DO NOT IGNORE GOODREADS

Goodreads: The Marketing Goldmine You're Ignoring

Most authors are obsessed with Amazon and Instagram while completely overlooking a platform where 125 million dedicated readers hang out daily. Goodreads isn't just another social media site—it's a community exclusively for people actively hunting for their next favorite book.

Consider this: 3.4 billion books added to shelves by people who visit the site for one purpose only—to find something new to read. They're not scrolling past cat videos or political rants. They're looking for you.

Many authors create a basic Goodreads profile and then abandon it, assuming it's "just a review site" or "too complicated." This mistake costs them thousands of potential readers. Goodreads sits earlier in the reader journey than

Amazon—it's where discovery happens before purchasing decisions are made.

Setting Up An Effective Goodreads Presence

The good news? Setting up an effective presence isn't complicated:

Your books deserve to find the readers who will treasure them. With its community of passionate book lovers already organized by genre preferences, Goodreads offers unmatched opportunities to connect with your ideal audience. Stop leaving this powerful platform untapped.

DO NOT EXPECT SIGNING SUCCESS WITHOUT PROMOTION

Beyond Traditional Bookstores

You don't need a prestigious bookstore to hold successful book signings. Community spaces, coffee shops, libraries, restaurants, farmers markets, craft fairs, schools, churches, and even fast-food venues like Chick-fil-A can serve as effective signing locations. The key isn't the prestige of the venue—it's the strategic promotion and audience connection that transforms any space into a successful signing opportunity.

The Empty Signing Reality

The mistake isn't the signing location. The mistake is assuming that the venue's newsletter announcement and poster will magically lure readers through the door. The mistake is thinking that simply being published is enough.

Book signings can be powerful—connections made, readers found, relationships forged with potential champions for your work. But they don't work by magic or wishful thinking. They work through deliberate, strategic promotion and realistic expectations.

Too many authors believe the field-of-dreams approach: if you sit at a signing table, readers will come. They won't. Not unless they know about it. Not unless they care. Not unless you've given them a reason to show up.

Creating Events Worth Attending

What pulls you out of your house on a weeknight? What makes you drive to a location rather than ordering online from your couch? It's not just the presence of an unknown author. It's the promise of an experience worth your precious time.

Successful signings require groundwork—connections built, audiences nurtured, expectations managed. Authors with packed signings didn't just announce the event. They created anticipation. They gave people a reason to care. They made their presence an occasion.

Before scheduling that signing, ask yourself: Who will come? How will they know about it? Why would they care? If your answers are vague hopes rather than concrete plans, you're not ready for that signing table.

Non-Traditional Signing Venues That Work

Consider these alternative signing locations:

- **Coffee Shops**: These community hubs often welcome authors, particularly during off-peak hours

- **Local Libraries**: Many have dedicated programs for local authors and built-in reader communities

- **Community Centers**: These offer connection to neighborhood residents and often support local talent

- **Specialty Retail Stores**: If your book aligns with their products (cookbooks in kitchen stores, gardening books in nurseries)

- **Art Galleries**: During openings or special events, particularly for visually rich books

- **Festivals and Fairs**: Where people are already gathered and in a mood to discover

- **School Events**: Particularly for children's, YA, or educational books

- **Professional Organization Meetings**: Where your expertise aligns with member interests

- **Restaurants**: During slower periods, especially if your book has a culinary or cultural connection

- **Wineries and Breweries**: Many host regular cultural events to drive traffic

The advantage of non-traditional venues is that they often come with built-in communities and may attract people who don't typically visit bookstores.

Understanding Venue Partnerships

Understand what any venue can and cannot do for you. They can provide space, include you in their calendar, perhaps mention you in promotional materials. They cannot build your audience. They cannot manufacture interest in your work. That's your job.

Start with your existing connections—friends, family, colleagues, social media followers, email subscribers. Personal invitations carry weight. A specific "I'm going to be at this location on this date and I'd love to see you there" brings more people than generic announcements.

Reach beyond your immediate circle. Contact local reading groups, writing organizations, or communities connected to your book's subject matter. Offer a short reading or discussion as part of your signing—something that adds value beyond just a signature.

The most successful signings aren't centered on the signing itself. They include a conversation, a reading followed by discussion, or a presentation about the book's subject. The signing becomes the closing ritual of a meaningful event.

Promotion Strategies That Fill Seats

- Create Facebook events and invite your network personally

- Send direct email invitations to your subscriber list

- Partner with the venue on cross-promotion

- Contact local media with a specific angle about your event

- Design eye-catching, shareable graphics for social media

DO NOT EXPECT SIGNING SUCCESS WITHOUT PROMOTION

- Offer a special incentive or gift for attendees
- Collaborate with other authors or local personalities
- Create a mini-workshop or presentation related to your book's theme
- Connect with relevant local groups whose members might be interested

Setting Realistic Expectations

Success doesn't always mean selling fifty books. Sometimes it means making five deep connections that lead to word-of-mouth recommendations. Sometimes it means building a relationship with a venue that welcomes you back. Sometimes it means getting comfortable with public speaking so your next event goes even better.

Measure success by growth, not just sales. Did you learn something? Did you connect with even one reader who truly appreciated your work? Did you become more comfortable talking about your book? These are victories worth celebrating.

The Reality of Modern Book Signings

In today's digital world, book signings aren't primarily about selling books—they're about creating experiences that can't be duplicated online. They're about the personal connection between author and reader. They're about building a community around your work.

The most successful authors approach signings as relationship-building opportunities rather than sales events. They understand that the true value often comes after the signing—in the reviews written, the recommendations shared, and the connections that lead to future opportunities.

With strategic planning, creative venue selection, and realistic expectations, book signings remain one of the most powerful tools in your author marketing arsenal. They simply require a new approach for a new era of publishing.

DO NOT IGNORE ANALYTICS

Let the Data Speak: What Your Readers Are Already Telling You

In the quiet glow of a laptop screen, the numbers stare back—columns of data stretching across the dashboard like an accusation. Six months of book marketing, thousands of words shared across platforms, dozens of newsletter issues sent into the void. All captured here, distilled into metrics many authors are too afraid to examine.

The analytics dashboard can quickly dampen creative enthusiasm. Open rates decline month after month, clicks become harder to find, and sales numbers? They soar at launch, only to plummet just as quickly. Every metric is a reflection of a reader's decision—to engage or move on, to invest or keep scrolling. The numbers don't lie, even when intuition hopes they might. They reveal a reality that a creative heart might resist, but a business mind must confront.

The Marketing Measurement Gap

Too many authors approach marketing as a creative endeavor disconnected from measurement. They craft posts, design graphics, write newsletters, and send them into the digital abyss with nothing but hope. They resist looking at the data, either from fear of what it might reveal or from a misguided belief that art shouldn't be reduced to metrics.

This resistance to analytics isn't artistic integrity—it's self-sabotage disguised as principle.

The digital landscape isn't merely a platform for expression; it's an ecosystem that speaks its own language. That language is data. Every click, every open, every purchase leaves a trace, a breadcrumb of reader behavior that, when followed, leads to understanding. When you ignore these signals, you're essentially blindfolded, stumbling through a marketplace you refuse to see.

What Analytics Actually Tell You

Analytics reveal which subject lines compel readers to open your emails and which send them reaching for the delete button. They show which social media posts generate engagement and which disappear without a ripple. They illuminate which price points trigger purchases and which create hesitation. This isn't abstract information—it's the direct voice of your potential readers telling you what resonates with them.

Consider this difference: One author publishes a newsletter, feels satisfied with the content, and moves on without examining the results. Another author notices that newsletters featuring behind-the-scenes content consistently achieve 40% higher open rates than promotional material. Which author will build the stronger reader connection over time?

The data doesn't diminish creativity—it directs it toward effectiveness.

The Tools You're Already Paying For

The marketing platforms you use already collect this information. Amazon provides impression and click data for your book page. Newsletter services track open rates and engagement patterns. Social media platforms offer insights into which content reaches your audience. These tools aren't collecting dust; they're gathering intelligence you're choosing to ignore.

Start with the Fundamentals

Track your basic sales patterns—not just quantities but timing. Do you sell more books on certain days of the week? Following specific marketing activities? At particular price points? These patterns reveal the rhythm of your readers' behavior, allowing you to time future efforts for maximum impact.

Examine your email metrics beyond the basic open rate. Which links do subscribers click most frequently? What time of day generates the highest engagement? Which segments of your audience respond to different types of content? The answers allow you to refine your approach with surgical precision rather than continuing to guess.

Study your website analytics to understand how readers find and interact with your online presence. Which pages do they visit most? How long do they stay? What path do they follow before purchasing—or before abandoning their journey? Each data point illuminates a moment of reader decision-making, a window into their experience with your brand.

Social media platforms offer particularly rich analytical landscapes, showing exactly which posts connect with your audience and which fall flat. The patterns often surprise even the most intuitive marketers. Content you believed would resonate might barely register, while seemingly minor posts sometimes trigger unexpected waves of engagement.

From Measurement to Strategy

The most powerful aspect of analytics isn't just measuring what happened—it's using that knowledge to predict and influence what happens next. When you understand that certain types of content consistently outperform others, you can strategically create more of what works. When you recognize that specific timing dramatically affects engagement, you can schedule accordingly. The data transforms marketing from hopeful broadcasting into strategic communication.

This approach requires humility. It means accepting that your instincts, however creative or well-intentioned, might not always align with reader preferences. It means acknowledging that the content you most enjoy creating might not be what your audience most enjoys consuming. This isn't about surrendering artistic control—it's about building a bridge between your creative vision and your readers' reality.

Make Analytics Manageable

Start small if the prospect feels overwhelming. Focus on one platform, one metric, one question you want to answer. Perhaps track open rates across different newsletter subject lines for a month. Or compare engagement between different types of social media content. The goal isn't to drown in data but to start listening to what it tells you.

Establish a regular review rhythm—perhaps monthly for comprehensive analysis, with weekly check-ins on current campaigns. The patterns only emerge with consistent attention over time. A single data point is merely an event; a series of data points becomes a trend worth responding to.

Embracing the Conversation

The analytics dashboard is not an accusation but a conversation—readers silently indicating their preferences, their habits, their desires. All you need to do is listen to what they're already telling you through their collective behavior.

Your marketing efforts deserve more than hope and intuition. They deserve the clarity that only data can provide. Your readers are already telling you what works through their engagement patterns—or lack thereof. The only question is whether you're willing to listen.

Ignoring analytics isn't protecting your creative process; it's refusing to hear the very audience you're trying to reach. Open yourself to what the data reveals, and watch as your marketing transforms from scattershot efforts into precision communication that truly connects with the readers waiting to discover your work.

DO NOT STOP MARKETING

The greatest tragedy in publishing isn't the book that fails to sell—it's the book that begins to succeed and then disappears because its author believed the work ended on launch day.

Many promising books vanish because authors treat marketing like a sprint instead of a marathon. They pour everything into that first week, celebrate their temporary Amazon ranking, then go silent—wondering why their sales plummet just as momentum was building. Meanwhile, they're missing critical promotional opportunities that could sustain and grow their success.

The Algorithm Factor and the Long Game

The algorithms controlling online visibility respond to consistent signals. Each marketing effort—a newsletter mention, social media post, or price promotion—creates ripples these algorithms detect. When those signals stop, your book begins its digital burial. No matter how strong your launch, silence afterward is a death sentence.

Think about how you discover books. Rarely does a single exposure trigger a purchase. Most readers need multiple touchpoints before buying. When your marketing disappears after launch, you eliminate those crucial secondary exposures that often trigger actual sales.

Strategic Promotional Opportunities You Can't Afford to Miss

Smart authors recognize that each phase of a book's life offers unique promotional angles:

Early months: Frequent touchpoints maintain momentum. Share reader reactions, celebrate milestones, continue conversations your book started. Use the "new release" window strategically—most retailers give extra visibility to books in their first 30-90 days.

Seasonal opportunities: Every genre has natural promotional cycles throughout the year. Romance novels spike around Valentine's Day. Financial books sell during tax season and the new year. Aligning your marketing pushes with these natural rhythms multiplies your effectiveness.

Backlist revival: As your catalog grows, strategic promotions of older titles can create ripple effects across your entire body of work. Price promotions on book one often drive full-price sales of later series entries.

Timely tie-ins: When your book's themes connect to current events, trending topics, or seasonal interests, you gain natural promotional angles. These "news hooks" create relevance that can open doors to media coverage, podcast interviews, and feature opportunities.

Identifying and Capitalizing on Strategic Moments

The most successful authors maintain a promotional calendar that identifies:

- Industry award submission deadlines
- Relevant holidays and seasonal themes
- Major genre conventions and events
- Retail promotion cycles (like Amazon's monthly deals)
- Topic-based promotional opportunities (National Mental Health Month, Financial Literacy Week, etc.)

When you systematically track these opportunities, you transform random marketing into strategic campaigns that reach readers at moments they're most receptive.

The Compound Effect of Consistent Marketing

Consistent marketing creates compound effects. Each blog mention builds on previous podcast appearances. Today's newsletter reinforces last month's social media campaign. Your book signing strengthens your online ads. These elements work together, creating an impression of momentum that attracts both algorithms and human attention.

Strategic consistency isn't mindless repetition. It means understanding the rhythm of effective book promotion—balancing direct sales appeals with relationship building, providing value while asking for support.

Beyond Social Media: Multi-Channel Promotional Strategy

Effective ongoing promotion extends beyond occasional social posts:

• **Email marketing:** Your most valuable asset for ongoing promotion. Consistent newsletters keep your book visible to your most engaged readers.

• **Content marketing:** Articles, blog posts, and videos related to your book's themes create discoverable paths back to your work.

• **Strategic price promotions:** Carefully timed discounts can revitalize sales and trigger algorithm boosts.

• **Advertising:** Targeted ads on retail platforms, social media, and reader sites maintain visibility between organic promotion.

• **Media outreach:** Connecting your book to current trends creates opportunities for interviews, guest posts, and features.

• **Cross-promotion:** Collaborating with other authors multiplies your reach without multiplying your workload.

Planning for Sustained Promotion Success

The difference between sporadic efforts and strategic promotion is planning:

1. Create a 12-month marketing calendar with key promotional opportunities mapped out
2. Develop a content bank of promotional assets you can deploy strategically
3. Establish sustainable systems that prevent marketing burnout
4. Focus on high-leverage activities that deliver the strongest results for your time investment
5. Track results to identify which promotional efforts drive actual sales

This approach transforms promotion from exhausting guesswork to sustainable strategy.

The Reality You Must Accept

Your book's journey doesn't end at publication—it begins. The authors who succeed long-term aren't necessarily the most talented writers—they're the ones who consistently show up after launch day, month after month, seizing promotional opportunities and maintaining visibility.

Your words deserved the care you took writing them. Your book deserves the commitment to keep it alive in the marketplace. Don't let it fade into digital obscurity after its brief moment in the spotlight.

Approach marketing as the marathon it truly is—one where consistency outperforms intensity, where strategic opportunity recognition trumps random effort, and where the ultimate winner isn't the fastest starter but the most persistent presence.

DO NOT MISS OPPORTUNITIES FOR FACE-TO-FACE PROMOTION

The empty booth looms like an accusation. Three hundred dollars spent on registration, another hundred on promotional materials, all for a laminated table and two folding chairs in a convention center's far corner. Passing crowds glance at neat stacks of unsold books, then continue toward bigger booths with flashier displays. Six hours into an eight-hour day, sales: exactly two books. Both to relatives who stopped by out of obligation.

This scene—this apparent failure—convinces many authors that book fairs aren't worth the investment. They retreat to online marketing, where rejection happens in silence. They convince themselves physical events are outdated expenses in a digital world, crossing them off their marketing list permanently.

And they're making a massive mistake.

The Unique Value of Physical Presence

Book fairs, literary festivals, and author events create opportunities digital marketing simply cannot replicate. They offer face-to-face connection in an increasingly distant marketplace. They provide credibility through association with established institutions. They create media opportunities rarely available to unknown authors. They build lasting relationships with booksellers, librarians, and readers who become advocates for your work.

Don't measure event success solely by day-of sales. Measure it by connections formed, visibility gained, and foundations laid for future growth.

The Different Nature of Physical Discovery

Think about how readers encounter your book online versus in person. Digital discovery happens in seconds—a quick glance at a cover, scan of reviews, instant decision. Physical discovery unfolds differently. Readers spend time with your book, feel its weight, open its pages. They meet you—the human behind the words.

Something fundamentally changes in this interaction—your book transforms from product to experience, and you transform from name to person. These encounters create readers who don't just purchase your book but champion it. They tell friends, "I met this author..." They recommend your work with the enthusiasm that comes from personal connection.

The value extends far beyond the immediate sale.

Strategic Exposure to Industry Gatekeepers

Events also offer strategic exposure to industry gatekeepers. Booksellers who might never notice your title among thousands in a distributor's catalog spend minutes discussing it with you. Librarians seeking new additions find you among curated exhibitors. Festival organizers witness your professionalism firsthand. Media covering these events discover new voices worth featuring.

Each conversation plants seeds that may germinate months later—the bookstore that adds your title to their local author section, the library that invites you for a reading, the festival that includes you in next year's programming.

Approaching Events Strategically

Successful authors approach events strategically, not haphazardly. Before committing, ask yourself:

- Does this event attract my target readership?

- Does it provide structured opportunities to connect with industry professionals?

- Does it offer programming that positions me as an expert?

- Does the investment align with my current career stage?

Preparation determines outcomes more than any other factor. Arrive with a compelling elevator pitch, professional materials, and clear objectives. The author who shows up unprepared, expecting the event itself to generate results without active participation, will find disappointment regardless of crowd size.

Understanding Attendee Psychology

Understand what attendees actually want. Readers don't attend book fairs to be sold to—they come for discovery, connection, and experience. Create visually interesting displays that invite conversation rather than demand purchase. Engage authentically rather than launching immediately into sales pitches. Offer something of value before expecting anything in return.

Your physical display communicates volumes. It should immediately tell people what genre you write, what readers can expect, and why they should stop to learn more. Professional signage, carefully arranged books, and thoughtfully designed promotional materials create credibility before you speak a word. A hastily assembled table signals that your work might be equally unpolished.

Maximizing Event Impact

Participate in programming to amplify your visibility. Panels, readings, workshops, and interviews position you as a voice worth hearing rather than merely a product. Attendees who encounter you first through your expertise become predisposed to explore your books afterward. This indirect approach often generates stronger results than direct selling.

The follow-up after events differentiates professionals from amateurs. Every card collected, contact made, or conversation initiated represents potential that requires nurturing. Send thoughtful follow-up messages, add new connections to your newsletter (with permission), and fulfill any promises made during the event. This transforms temporary visibility into lasting relationship.

Finding Value in Every Experience

Even seemingly unsuccessful events offer value. The quiet periods give you opportunities to connect with fellow authors who become valuable sources of information and future collaboration. The booth that attracted few visitors still generated photographs for social media, demonstrating your professional commitment. The conversations with the handful of engaged readers provided insights into how your book resonates—information nearly impossible to gather online.

Evaluate financial investments realistically against your career stage. Early-career authors might prioritize local events while established authors with multiple titles can justify larger investments in national expositions. Regional book festivals often provide the most balanced opportunity—professional credibility without the extreme costs of major trade shows.

The Power of Consistency

Consistency builds momentum. Your first local book festival might generate modest results, but your third appearance creates recognition among regular attendees. Your name on multiple event programs builds credibility with industry professionals who notice your persistent presence. Attending once then declaring it worthless misses the cumulative value that develops through repeated participation.

Digital and physical promotion should complement each other. Events generate content for your online platforms. In-person connections strengthen your digital network. Physical presence enhances your online authority. Authors who thrive understand this synergy rather than choosing one approach exclusively.

The landscape continues evolving, with hybrid models emerging that combine physical presence with digital reach. Virtual components extend the impact of in-person events, connecting you with readers beyond geographical limitations. Monitor these developments and adapt your approach to maximize exposure while managing resources effectively.

Your words deserve to be discovered. Your books merit the deeper connection that happens when readers encounter both the work and its creator. Your career benefits from the credibility, visibility, and relationships that only physical presence can cultivate.

The path to readers extends beyond the digital landscape into the physical world where lasting impressions form and genuine connections flourish. Walk that path with strategic purpose, and watch your author career develop dimensions impossible to achieve through pixels alone.

VIII. MINDSET & BUSINESS GROWTH MISTAKES

DO NOT FORGET YOU'RE BUILDING A CAREER

Beyond Comparison and One-Hit Wonders: Creating a Sustainable Author Journey

The midnight glow of your screen illuminates a landscape of comparison—social media posts celebrating six-figure book deals, newsletter screenshots of bestseller rankings, conference photos of authors whose names you've admired for years. Each image strikes like a physical blow. Your single published book sits quietly on your desk, its modest sales figures and handful of reviews suddenly seeming worthless.

Meanwhile, the manuscript for your second book sits untouched, victim to the paralyzing thought: "Why bother? I'll never match their success."

This crushing weight of comparison and the dangerous belief that one book is enough have claimed more writing careers than rejection ever could.

The Comparison Trap That Destroys Careers

What we witness of others' journeys is carefully curated—the highlight reel that hides years of struggle, failure, and persistence.

That author announcing their breakthrough deal today? They wrote five unpublished manuscripts over a decade before this one. The writer celebrating their bestseller status launched three previous books that barely covered production costs. The novelist whose social media presence radiates confidence nearly abandoned writing multiple times before finding their voice.

You're comparing your unfiltered experience—complete with every doubt, setback, and struggle—against others' perfectly edited public narratives. It's not comparing apples to oranges; it's comparing your entire orchard, including the diseased trees and failed crops, to someone else's hand-picked fruit basket.

Comparison serves no productive purpose. It cannot improve your writing or expand your audience. It only drains the energy you need for creating, learning, and persisting. Each moment spent measuring your journey against another's is a moment stolen from actually walking your own path.

Beyond the First Book: Building a Sustainable Career

The manuscript sits on your desk, polished after countless drafts. Your cover gleams from the screen, title rendered in carefully chosen typography. Launch day approaches—terrifying and exhilarating. After months or years of work, your book is about to enter the world.

This moment feels like an ending. The conclusion of a creative marathon. The fulfillment of a dream.

It's not. It's barely the starting line.

The most dangerous myth in publishing isn't about craft or marketing—it's the seductive belief that one book is enough. That a single title can establish a career, build an audience, generate sustainable income, or fully express your vision. This myth has killed more promising careers than any rejection ever could.

Publishing success demands a catalog, not a single title. The economics, algorithms, reader relationships, and career momentum all depend on continued production.

The Cold, Hard Numbers of Multiple Books

A single title—even one that sells well—rarely generates enough revenue to sustain a writing life. Your income gets divided across years of creation, production, and marketing. Calculate that hourly wage honestly, and you'll likely weep. The financial equation only begins to make sense when multiple titles share the burden of generating income.

Modern publishing platforms actively reward prolific authors. Amazon's algorithms favor consistent publishers, showing preference to authors with multiple titles and regular releases. Each new book becomes a discovery point for your entire catalog. A reader who finds your third book often purchases your first and second, creating revenue from work completed years ago.

Today's readers don't just connect with individual books—they invest in relationships with authors they trust. They want to know that discovering you means finding not just one good read, but a doorway to many. An author with a single title appears risky—someone who may never produce again—while multiple books represent a reliable source of continued engagement.

The Path Forward: Building Your Author Career

Instead of looking outward for validation, develop internal metrics. What specific aspects of craft have you improved since your last project? How has your understanding of narrative structure deepened? In what ways has your marketing become more effective? These questions generate actionable insights rather than paralyzing comparison.

Your unique voice deserves to develop according to its own organic timeline. Some writers find their stride immediately; others require multiple books to realize their potential. Some stories demand years of personal growth before you're ready to tell them effectively.

The only truly meaningful comparison is between your past and present self. Are you writing with more clarity than before? Have you developed stronger instincts for story structure? Has your dialogue become more nuanced? These questions generate productive reflection rather than destructive comparison.

The path forward becomes clear only when you stop looking sideways.

Creating Momentum Through Multiple Books

Think career, not book. Planning a writing career rather than a single book changes your approach to everything. You begin thinking in terms of sustainable systems rather than one-time efforts. You invest in skills, relationships, and platforms that serve you across multiple projects. Success metrics extend beyond single-title performance to catalog development, audience growth, and career longevity.

The "breakout book" phenomenon deserves reconsideration too. What appears as a single title suddenly catching fire typically represents the culmination of audience-building across previous works. That "overnight success" usually happens with an author's third, fourth, or tenth book, when accumulated readership reaches critical mass.

For those who fear they lack ideas for multiple books, remember that creativity expands through practice. The more you write, the more possibilities you discover. Completing one book often reveals threads that lead to the next. Characters demand their own stories. Themes require deeper exploration. The blank page becomes less intimidating with each project completed.

Your Foundation Stone

Your first book represents a tremendous accomplishment worthy of celebration. It proves you can transform ideas into completed work. But viewing it as a destination rather than a waypoint limits its potential impact. Seeing it instead as the foundation of a developing body of work opens possibilities a single volume cannot contain.

Successful authors in every genre share one fundamental characteristic: they kept writing. They understood that each book built upon the last, that audience development happens across multiple titles, and that financial sustainability requires a catalog rather than a single product.

Your story doesn't end with this book—it's just beginning. The readers you reach, skills you develop, and systems you build all create the foundation for what comes next. The question isn't whether your first book succeeds by whatever metric you've established. The question is whether you'll continue creating beyond it, building something larger than any single volume could contain.

Keep writing. Your second book becomes stronger for having completed the first. Your third benefits from lessons learned in both previous works. Your audience grows, your craft deepens, and your voice strengthens—but only if you continue.

One book can be a milestone. Only multiple books can build a career.

The publishing landscape rewards the author who plants forests, not just trees—who builds sustainable ecosystems of work rather than focusing on single-title performance. Your words deserve patient cultivation. Your creative vision warrants the sustained commitment that builds a career rather than merely launching books.

Patient persistence remains publishing's most powerful strategy.

DO NOT AVOID AUTHOR NETWORKING

The writing life looks solitary from the outside—just you battling your manuscript in isolation. In reality, while writing itself demands focused alone time, building a successful author career requires community. Full stop.

Too many authors—especially introverts—actively resist networking with other writers. Some fear competition. Others worry about measuring up. Many believe they should just focus on writing. This resistance is killing your career before it starts.

The Lone Writer Myth Is Destroying Your Potential

The publishing industry is an interconnected ecosystem, not a collection of isolated creators. Every successful author stands on the shoulders of peers who offered advice, opened doors, shared opportunities, and helped them survive the inevitable disappointments.

When you examine any bestselling author's journey closely, you'll find writer friends who read early drafts, suggested agents, made editor introductions, or provided emotional lifelines during rejection. What looks like individual success is almost always a community achievement behind the scenes.

For self-published authors, community isn't optional—it's survival. Traditional publishers help with marketing, distribution, and guidance. Independent authors must build these systems themselves. Doing this alone isn't just harder—it's nearly impossible.

What Author Networks Actually Provide

Real-Time Industry Intelligence

Publishing evolves constantly—algorithms change overnight, yesterday's marketing tactics fail today, and new opportunities appear without announcement. No individual can track all these changes, but communities collectively monitor everything that matters.

When Amazon overhauls its ad system, someone in your network catches it first and shares insights. When a new promotion method shows promise, community members test it and report back. These information flows keep you from operating blindfolded in a constantly shifting landscape.

Marketing Reach Beyond Your Dreams

Even a small author network exponentially extends your marketing reach. Cross-promotion creates one of the most powerful discovery systems in publishing. Newsletter swaps, joint promotions, boxed sets, anthology contributions, and social shares all work better in community.

These collaborative efforts succeed because readers trust author recommendations. When a writer they enjoy suggests another author's book, that endorsement carries weight that advertising dollars can't buy. These warm introductions consistently outperform cold marketing approaches.

Emotional Support When You're Ready to Quit

Publishing delivers brutal emotional swings—acceptance highs followed by crushing feedback, release day excitement followed by crickets. These rollercoasters break many aspiring authors. Only fellow writers truly understand these experiences.

When your launch underperforms, author friends provide perspective from similar experiences. When a harsh review hits, writer communities remind you that criticism comes with the territory. This emotional support prevents countless authors from abandoning their careers during inevitable rough patches.

Career Opportunities You'd Never Find Alone

Writers hear about opportunities through other writers—anthology invitations, speaking gigs, teaching positions, promotional features, even agent introductions often travel through author networks before becoming public. These opportunities rarely reach isolated authors.

Conference organizers ask existing speakers for recommendations. Anthology editors reach out to writers they know. Connected writers hear about these opportunities first and often receive the personal recommendation that seals the deal.

Building Author Connections That Actually Matter

Start Small and Real

Effective networking doesn't require attending major conferences or collecting hundreds of shallow connections. Begin with genuine engagement in manageable communities:

- Genre-specific Facebook groups
- Local writing organizations
- Online forums like Reddit's writing communities
- Twitter conversations around writing hashtags
- Virtual or local critique groups

Focus initially on learning and contributing rather than self-promotion. Ask good questions, celebrate others' wins, and share useful information. These authentic interactions build meaningful connections that transactional networking never will.

Find Your People

Not every author group will fit you. Seek communities matching your:

- Genre and category

- Publishing approach (traditional, indie, hybrid)
- Career stage and ambitions
- Communication style and values
- Specific challenges (balancing writing with parenting, health issues, day jobs)

The most valuable connections often come from writers slightly ahead of you on similar paths. They understand your current challenges while offering perspective from recent experience.

Give First, Ask Later

The most connected authors establish themselves as generous community members long before making requests. Contribute to conversations, celebrate others' successes, share resources, offer feedback, and promote books you genuinely enjoy.

When you eventually need beta readers, blurbs, or promotional support, people will remember your previous generosity. The author who only appears when needing something quickly burns through community goodwill.

Create Structured Relationships

Beyond casual online interaction, develop more structured connections:

- Critique partnerships for manuscript feedback
- Accountability groups for writing goals
- Marketing masterminds for promotional strategies
- Mentorship relationships with experienced authors

- Co-writing partnerships for collaborative projects

These structured relationships often evolve into deeper professional partnerships, providing consistent support and collaboration.

Overcoming Your Networking Resistance

For Introverts

Introverts often thrive in author networking despite initial resistance. The writing community contains many introverts who understand the need for space and meaningful connection. Consider:

- Starting with text-based communities rather than video calls
- Focusing on one-to-one relationships before group settings
- Scheduling limited, focused networking time with recovery periods
- Leveraging your listening skills as a networking strength

Many successful author communities operate primarily online, allowing you to participate from home when your energy permits.

For Those Fearing Competition

Other authors aren't your competition. Readers who enjoy your work typically read multiple authors in your genre. When readers finish a book they love, they seek similar experiences, not identical ones.

The most successful authors regularly promote peers who write similar books because:

- It builds reciprocity (others promote their work in return)
- It positions them within a genre community readers recognize
- It demonstrates confidence in their unique voice
- It creates larger collective visibility for their category

The author who fears recommending similar books fundamentally misunderstands reader psychology.

For Those Feeling Intimidated

Many writers believe they have nothing to offer established authors. This ignores the reciprocal nature of author relationships and the value newer writers bring:

- Fresh perspectives and enthusiasm
- Knowledge from other professional backgrounds
- Social media skills older authors may lack
- Responsiveness and availability that busier authors can't match
- Future support as their own careers develop

Most established authors remember who helped them and willingly support emerging writers. The publishing community sustains itself through this ongoing cycle of mutual support.

Setting Boundaries That Protect Your Writing

While community provides essential support, balance remains critical:

- Schedule specific times for networking separate from writing sessions
- Learn to say no to opportunities that don't align with your priorities
- Create social media boundaries that prevent constant distraction
- Limit critique partner commitments to what you can genuinely fulfill
- Step back from toxic community dynamics immediately

Effective author communities understand these boundaries and respect members' need to prioritize creation first.

The Ultimate Benefit: Career Insurance

Beyond immediate advantages, author communities provide essential career longevity. Publishing careers span decades, during which:

- Retailers rise and fall
- Publishing houses merge or close
- Genres evolve or transform

- Marketing platforms change dramatically

- Personal circumstances shift unexpectedly

Authors with strong communities navigate these shifts successfully, while isolated writers often get crushed. When a publisher closes, connected authors receive referrals to new opportunities. When personal crisis interrupts writing, community members help maintain visibility. When markets change, networked authors learn adaptations quickly.

Your author community represents your most valuable long-term professional asset—more important than any single book, contract, or marketing tactic. It provides the collective wisdom, emotional support, and collaborative opportunities that sustain careers through publishing's inevitable disruptions.

The writing itself demands solitude, but building a sustainable author career requires community. Don't let introversion, intimidation, or misplaced competitive thinking keep you from the connections that will amplify your work for years to come.

THE END

DO NOT SAY "THE END" IF YOU'RE NOT FINISHED

If you've made it this far, congratulations. You've survived my unfiltered take on what it really takes to succeed in self-publishing. No sugar-coating. No false promises. Just the hard-earned truth from someone who's been in the trenches.

I've watched countless talented writers publish books that never found their audience. Not because the writing wasn't good enough, but because they refused to treat publishing like the business it is. They clung to the romantic notion that great writing alone would carry them to success.

It won't. Great writing matters tremendously. But in today's crowded marketplace, it's the starting point, not the finish line.

The Self-Publishing Paradox

The greatest irony of self-publishing is that success comes when you take the "self" out of the equation. Your personal preferences, your convenience, your comfort zone—all must take a backseat to what actually works.

Successful indie authors aren't just writers. They're publishers. Marketers. Entrepreneurs. Business owners. They make decisions based on market realities, not personal convenience. They invest in professionalism, not shortcuts. They build systems, not just books.

This isn't about selling out. It's about showing up professionally in an industry that demands it.

What I Hope You've Learned

Throughout this guide, I've hammered home the essentials:

- Professional editing isn't optional—it's the foundation of credibility
- Cover design must meet industry standards for your genre—no exceptions
- Book descriptions sell books more effectively than the writing inside
- Email lists are your most valuable marketing asset—build yours relentlessly
- Strategic metadata determines whether readers find your book at all
- Distribution beyond a single platform protects your long-term career
- Author community provides the connections that create opportunities
- Pricing strategy affects both perception and profitability

- Marketing isn't something you do after publishing—it's integrated from day one
- Consistent publishing builds momentum that sporadic releases never achieve

After the Book Closes

What happens next is entirely up to you.

Some of you will take this information and transform your publishing approach. You'll invest in quality, build sustainable systems, and approach your writing career with newfound professionalism. Your books will find their audience, and your work will make the impact it deserves.

Others will continue as before—publishing books without proper editing, slapping together DIY covers, avoiding marketing, and wondering why success remains elusive.

The path you choose determines everything.

Failure and Success

Most self-published books fail. That's just statistical reality. They sell fewer than 100 copies lifetime and fade into digital obscurity.

But here's what publishing gurus won't tell you: These failures aren't random. They're predictable. They follow patterns of avoidable mistakes—the very ones I've outlined in this book.

The authors who succeed aren't necessarily more talented writers. They're simply more professional publishers. They respect the craft of writing and the business of books equally.

They make decisions based on market realities, not wishful thinking.

My Challenge to You

As we close this journey together, I offer one final challenge:

Choose one area where you've been cutting corners. Just one. Maybe it's cover design. Maybe it's marketing. Maybe it's building your email list. Make a commitment today to elevate your standards in that single area.

Not tomorrow. Not when you have more money or time. Today.

This small shift in approach—from amateur to professional, from hopeful to strategic—changes everything. It signals to yourself and the market that you're serious about your work. That you respect your readers enough to deliver excellence. That you value your words enough to give them their best chance to succeed.

The Next Chapter Is Yours

I've given you everything I know about what works and what doesn't in self-publishing. I've shared the mistakes that have cost authors thousands of dollars and countless missed opportunities. I've outlined the strategies that transform struggling writers into successful author-entrepreneurs.

The rest is up to you.

Your words deserve to be read. Your stories deserve to find

their people. Your message deserves to make its impact. But deserving isn't enough. It never has been.

Taking the "self" out of self-publishing means approaching every decision as a professional publisher would—with strategy, market awareness, and unwavering commitment to quality. It means building a business around your creativity, not just hoping your creativity will somehow find its way in the world.

This is the path to sustainable success. Not quick wins or viral luck, but steady, strategic growth built on a foundation of professionalism and persistence.

I believe your work is worth this effort. I believe your readers are waiting to discover you. I believe your publishing journey can be everything you hope—if you're willing to approach it with the seriousness it demands.

Now go publish something remarkable. The world needs your words—professionally packaged, strategically positioned, and powerfully promoted.

I'll be cheering you on from the sidelines.

www.ingramcontent.com/pod-product-compliance
Lightning Source LLC
Chambersburg PA
CBHW050336010526
44119CB00049B/573